One Singer
One Song

One Singer
One Song

Songs Of Glasgow Folk

Ewan McVicar

Illustrations by John Gahagan

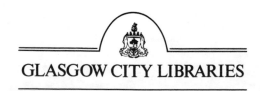

GLASGOW CITY LIBRARIES

For my father, who would have liked to read it, for Linda, who helped make it, and for Norrie Buchan, who helped me learn how and why.

Text © Ewan McVicar, 1990.
Illustrations by John Gahagan, 1990.
Music transcribed by Ewan McVicar, 1990.

ISBN 0-906169-31-3

Published by Glasgow City Libraries, The Mitchell Library, North Street, Glasgow G3 7DN.

In accordance with the 'One Singer One Song' principle the music was transcribed by the author on computer, and printed by Smallbiz, 142 Queen Margaret Drive, Glasgow G20 8NY.

The text design was worked out on a DTP programme, then supplied on floppy disc, with the author's design layout notes, to Bell and Bain Ltd, 303 Burnfield Road, Thornliebank, Glasgow G46 7UQ, who originated and printed the book.

CONTENTS

I have omitted some very well known and widely printed songs—'Red Yo Yo', 'I Belong To Glasgow', 'The Jeely Piece Song'—preferring to use some songs that should be better known or fit my theme better, and I've chosen songs which I associate with individual singers, not with groups.

I've chosen songs that express something of the energy, pithiness, gallusness and humour of Glasgow. Songs that remind us of Glasgow's past—the hardship or the human warmth, the victories or defeats for the people, the small details of daily living, the landmarks that progress is tearing down.

My singing connection with the songs of Glasgow came through my involvement in folk music, so my songs of Glasgow mostly have a strong folk song connection.

When I first began singing in public folk songs were things you learned in school, and forgot as you went out the gate. Then what has been called the Folk Song Revival happened. This book tells some of the story of how that happened, and the singers and songwriters involved.

I talk about singers who wrote some of these songs. Singers who have given new life to old songs, who have made new songs widely known. Or who are just one part of the process of keeping song writing and singing a live event in Glasgow, not something only to be listened to passively through a loudspeaker or earphones.

Over the past twenty years the term folk song has been devalued, but the songs and ways of singing them that excited me and a few others in the late 1950s have been readopted by the people.

Don't read this book thinking of folk songs as something foreign, to do with Aran sweaters or Joan Baez, John Denver or Donovan, songs about knights or cowboys or ploughboys.

Yes, there are wonderful folk songs about such people and subjects. But the folk songs here are about people who live and have lived in Glasgow, written by people who live or have lived in Glasgow. (I have squeezed in a few from greater Glasgow, including Milngavie, Clydebank and Rutherglen.)

Without trying to define what a 'folk song' is in present-day Glasgow, nearly every song you find in this book is one I have heard sung in a folk setting in Glasgow—a folk club, pub, party or concert.

You may know the song but think I've made a mistake in the lyrics.

Remember these songs undergo a continuous process of change. The singer learns them inexactly, often learning songs third-hand from someone who has already changed them from the composer's intention, then unconsciously making alterations in the course of singing.

This is not laziness or wilfulness. It's a process which has always happened to folk songs.

A song which has passed through several transfers will have altered markedly. Sometimes the dross of uninteresting verses has been filtered out, sometimes a skilful phrase has been turned into gibberish by a singer who didn't listen closely. Unless I could find out the original way the song was made, I have chosen what seem to me the 'best' versions—that is, the ones which make the most sense to me while retaining the most attractive features of melody and phrasing.

The attraction of the songs in this book is not just in the sense they make. Sometimes it is the way words and tune interact. Sometimes the charm is in the way the song evokes the feelings of people involved in an event. Sometimes it is the only record we have of the people's view of a happening or period. Sometimes the song challenges the orthodox views of life in an interesting way.

Where I can find a version showing how the writer of the song intended it, I've used that, even if the song is now well-known in the version of a particular singer—it is hard to make a good song, and the original maker has the right to show his or her intention.

That is why you'll find several ways of rendering Scots or Glesga (or Glesca or even Glesgie for that matter) speech on the page. I consulted the writer or the most authoritative version, and used that version. I prefer not to show a rainfall of apostrophes representing 'missing' letters that were never in the Scots language, and have never understood the life and feeding habits of the semi-colon, but if the songwriter wants them, that suits me.

One of the songwriters in this book, Andy Hunter, pointed out recently that when he and I were growing up the kind of songs that interested and excited us could not be heard on radio or TV. It was so hard to find this music we suspected that to enjoy it was vaguely subversive and possibly illegal—the way Acid House is at the time of writing.

Now the folk and roots music of the whole wide world is available through your local record shop, there are daily helpings on radio of quality Scottish music, and performers and bands tour the world performing Scots traditional music and song.

More, songs that were known only to and kept alive by a handful of singers are now part of everyone's Scotland—'Ye Canny Shove Yer Grannie', 'The Bonny Lass O Fyvie', 'Wild Mountain Thyme'. (Yes, I know the last one is Irish, but a lot of people think it is Scots. Anyway, it is based on 'The Braes Of Balquidder', a song by Paisley poet Robert Tannahill.)

More yet, Burns based his songwriting squarely on the traditional songs he found around him, using and adapting tunes and formats, adding new verses and collating differing versions he heard. That approach has been revitalised by the songwriters who participated and helped to shape the Folk Revival that began in the 1950s. They learned from and added to the tradition so well that some of the composed songs in this book regularly turn up credited to 'trad' on records.

Many of the singers and songwriters in this book share credit for helping create the revival and revitalisation of Scottish song. Glasgow played a major role in that revival.

'He'll hold you with his charms'

The Star Club in Berkeley Street

Carol Laula - STANDING PROUD
Jim McKenna - SCREW'S BARLINNIE BLUES
Archie Fisher - SHIPYARD APPRENTICE
Cilla Fisher - CANNY SHOVE YER GRANNIE,
HAIRY MARY, I WILL IF YOU WILL
Alasdair Robertson - KELVINGROVE
Arthur Johnstone - THE JOHN MACLEAN MARCH
Iain Ingram - ANNIE MCKELVIE

'HE'LL HOLD YOU WITH HIS CHARMS'

The singers who created the Glasgow Folk Revival are hard to find.

Some have moved away, some are dead, many are on the move—earning a living from music.

Those still in Glasgow have few places where they can perform—the pubs prefer bands. There are even fewer places where the non-professional songwriters in this book can be enquired for. The folk clubs of yesteryear have evaporated like snaw aff a dyke.

One folk club has kept a platform and a microphone open through the lean times.

The Star Club opened in 1978. For some years it met in the Star Social Club on the south bank of the Clyde facing over to the city centre. Then it moved north to Berkeley Street, into the Society of Musicians social club.

The Star Club is the creation and the achievement of Arthur Johnstone.

Arthur's determination, his principle of mixing famous and new performers, his preparedness to let anyone who asks sing (provided they are early enough in the queue), his own fine distinctive unaccompanied voice, and his commitment to songs—some of social comment, people's history, but many just great singing songs—all of these give the Star a special sense of identity.

The link between song and social or political comment is for Arthur the essence of folk music.

'Really, folk music is telling you what happened at certain times in the past. It's the one way we have available of handing down history. A song we knew as a new song twenty years ago can now be recognised as a part of the tradition, telling something about the life and happenings of Glasgow.'

On a normal night in the Star Arthur will himself begin the night with a favourite song or two. Perhaps Matt McGinn's 'Benny Lynch'. Or John McCreadie's 'Doomsday In The Afternoon', Hamish Henderson's 'John MacLean March'. Or even 'Drumchapel Mist'.

> A purple flush comes over yer cheeks and spreads down to yer toes.
> Your teeth play castanets inside yer jaw and yer tongue comes down yer nose.
> Gallacher's famous homemade wine easily gets you pissed.
> If you wake up in the morning you'll rue the day you drank Drumchapel Mist.

14

Then you may find a nervous new 'floor singer', perhaps on their first time of singing to an audience. He or she may be singing their own composition or a song new to him or her which the audience has grown weary of.

A new singer's enthusiasm will probably reactivate positive feeling for an old song—and they'll join in the chorus anyway, to help the singer along.

The new hand may be followed by a veteran like Jim Brown trying out his latest composition on his friends. It may be serious social comment. It may be a nostalgic song about the shipyards, wry humour about the football pools or straight political polemic.

Then the guest act of the evening comes on. Only one advertised, only one receiving a fee. (The other performers will get their entrance money back, though.) It may be a solo singer, a group, an instrumentalist. Scots Irish, English, much further afield. It was in the Star I heard Tomas Lynch, an Irishman, sing 'My Song Of The Clyde', written by a Scot living in Germany.

'Part of running a club is not just to put on popular artists,' Arthur Johnstone believes, 'but to give an opportunity to other good artists who are about, who will become more popular as people hear them.'

The Star is popular with singers. Noted folk performers from Ireland or the Continent will base tours of Scotland around the dates available to them to play at the Star.

The club runs on licensed premises of course—folk song seems to have wedded the bottle, although the first folk concerts and clubs in Glasgow were quite happy in boozeless venues.

There is an irony in such a stronghold of traditional song and support for the truly amateur singer meeting in the hallowed halls of the Society of Musicians Club, complete with busts of Beethoven and Bach and portraits of former Glasgow musical worthies.

I fear those worthies—gents one and all—would have considered the Star Club's music to be the sweepings of the street and the despised music hall. Where are their own august and weighty compositions now? Hiding in the dusty library files. The other invigorator of the hallowed Society hall is that close relative of folk music, jazz.

Jazz, apparently all improvisation, usually turns out on closer inspection to be mostly arrangements with solos which are first worked out as improvisations, but then repeated and restructured when the tune is played again.

15

Folk, apparently all repetition by rote, usually turns out on closer inspection to be mostly rearrangements with subtle variations of songs as learned from other performers, with a large mixture of songwriters singing their own compositions which use the common elements of what is allowed to wear the 'folksong' label. Often they are more lyric writers than songwriters, using the wealth of traditional tunes.

In Glasgow folk song, and most especially in that area where song is used in Glasgow for comment on immediate social issues, the words seem to be of more importance than the tune. Only two of the songs in this book have to my knowledge had other tunes fitted to the words—'Nancy Whisky' and 'The Auchengeich Disaster'—while a good half of the songs are words bolted on to tunes that started life elsewhere.

Sometimes there is a joke contained in recognising the original words.

Billy Connolly wrote, to the tune of 'Last Train To San Fernando',

> Last train to Glasgow Central. Last train to Glasgow Central.
> I'll be hidin in the lavvy when the ticket man comes,
> Beedy beedy bare bum, to Glasgow Central.

How about this?

> We came on a thirty three, ma mammy and me.
> Round all the shops we did roam.
> We spent and we spent till our cards got bent,
> Ah feel so fed up, ah wanny go home.
> Ah hate the Glasgow sales, ah hate the things ah bought,
> Ah'd like tae chuck the lot and just go home.
> Come on, bus thirty three, ah'll sit on somebody's knee.
> Ah feel so fed up, ah wanny go home.

How quickly did you spot the 'Sloop John B'?
Then there is 'One Man Went To Mow', altered to

> Three men frae Carntyne went tae jine the Parish.
> Three men frae Carntyne and a bottle of wine, went tae jine the Parish.
> ('Jine the Parish' of course translates into 'apply for Income Support from the DSS.')

This song was originated by someone in Dunfermline, I believe, and was some three verses long. Fife singer John Watt heard it and added to it, Iain Mackintosh took it further into Glesga and added more verses again, then Billy Connolly made it famous.

Iain's last verse is

> Three men frae Carntyne, a bottle of wine, five Woodbine, a big black greyhound dug called Boab, frae up oor close, alang oor street, and wee Agnes oot the dairy who's been skelly ever since a Milanda boy hit her on the heid wi a breid board and went out and didny shut the door and forgot tae apologise, went tae jine the Parish.
> And it was shut.

The explosion of peace songs in the early 60s all reused tunes from elsewhere. This system is still used by the Scottish CND Buskers, based in Glasgow and the West. Consider the following.

> If your country's won the war, and ye want tae cheer,
> Go up tae the surface and order up a beer.
> You find there's no much company, the place is looking bare.
> Just stey doon in the shelter underneath the stair.
> Doon in the shelter, underneath the stair.
> Everybody's dirty, everybody's bare.
> And we huvnae got much culture, we huvnae got much hair,
> Doon in the shelter underneath the stair.
> (By Ian Davison to the tune of 'Doon In The Wee Room'.)

> Make sure your front door's locked and your drains aint blocked.
> Turn your gas off too if you want to live through.
> Make sure that there's enough water and stuff to keep you all alive.
> Through the time of radiation. Expect complete annihilation.
> There will be no consolation
> From the Government's Protect And Survive.
> (By Pat Plunkett to the tune of 'The Hokey Cokey'.)

This use and abuse of tunes dates back long before the peace movement. What are called Glasgow Street songs are invariably to borrowed melodies. Like 'Yankee Doodle'.

> A wee bird cam tae oor ha door, ah thocht it wis a sparra,
> For it began tae whistle up the tune they cry O'Hara.
> Ah threw the bird a thruppenny bit—ah didny think ah hud yin.
> The wee bird wudny pick it up because it wis a dud yin.
> Rab Tamson wis a sporty blade, he bet a man a fiver
> That he could loup Jamaica Bridge like Rabbie Burns the Diver.
> The folk that stood aroond the bridge kicked up an awfu shindy
> Fur Jock fell doon the tunnel of the Clutha Number Twenty.

(The Cluthas were ferry boats some of which later became pleasure steamers. For younger readers, a thruppenny was a quarter of a shilling, an old form of currency. I have an unprovable theory that Rabbie Burns became a diver as a result of inflation, and that the bet used to be a pound, referred to as a note or 'no-ate' which rhymes with Rabbie Burns the Po-ate. On the other hand, there is always a lump of prosaic fact about. Moyna Gardner tells me there was a Willy Burns, famous for having dived off Jamaica Street Bridge!)

'The British Grenadiers' is used for

> Ma Aunty Jean frae Glesga came alang wi ma Aunty Jenny.
> She pit her hand intae her purse and gied me a brand new penny.
> Ah ran tae the shop tae buy some rock and ah met wi wee O'Hara.
> He says 'Gie me a sook o yer rock and ah'll gi ye a hurl in ma barra.'
> Oh, the bonny wee barra's mine, it doesny belang tae O'Hara.
> The fly wee bloke, he's stuck tae ma rock, noo ah'm gonny stick tae his barra.

Sometimes you recognise the tune but cannot name it.

> When ah wis single, ah used tae comb ma hair.
> Noo ah'm married ah huvnae the time tae spare.
> It's a life, a life, a weary weary life.
> Ye're better tae be single than tae be a married wife.
> When ah wis single ah used a powder puff.
> Noo that ah'm married ah canny afford the stuff.
> Fur one says 'Mammy, help me oot o ma pram'.
> Anither says 'Mammy, gies a piece an jam'.
> One says 'Mammy, help me intae ma bed'.
> Anither says 'Mammy, scratch ma wooden leg'.
> It's a life, a life, a weary weary life.
> Ye're better tae be single than tae be a married wife.

The middle part of 'Fare Thee Well For I Must Leave You' turns into

> Ah've a laddie in America,
> Ah've anither in Dundee-ah-ee-ah-ee.
> Ah've anither in Australia,
> And that's the one who's gaun tae marry me-ah-ee-ah-ee.
> First he took me tae America,
> Then he took me tae Dundee-ah-ee-ah-ee.
> Then he ran away and left me
> Wi three bonny bairnies on my knee-ah-ee-ah-ee.
> One wis sittin by the fireside.
> One wis sittin on my knee-ah-ee-ah-ee.
> One wis standin in the door way
> Singin 'Daddy, Daddy, please come back tae me-ah-ee-ah-ee.'

Aw the sad!

The folk songs of Glasgow are by no means all just an ecologically sound recycling of old melodies. Half the song tunes I print here are either original or so altered it takes a specialist to diagnose the original condition.

The Star Club is the premier venue of a handful of places you might find these songs and singers—The Scotia, The Babbity Bowster, the Riverside Club, Heilan Jessie's. During the Glasgow Tryst in November or the Folk Festival in July there is a more concentrated gathering of performers.

The shortage of performance places doesn't slow down the rate at which people write.

If you want to jam up your letter box, insert a paragraph in a Glasgow paper suggesting you just might be seeking new songs.

If you add 'Poems that someone could set to music also welcome' you'll need a shovel to get out of your front door.

People will phone you to sing songs. They'll demand to come round and play them to you. They'll humbly ask your opinion, then send you fifteen new songs on any subject you suggest.

The songs are everywhere. Add to this year's new ones the thousands composed last year. This book is just a taster. Most of the songwriters have a dozen more songs just as good. I've tried to choose the most Glesga in language or topic, some of the best loved and some of the best new ones.

Let us begin.

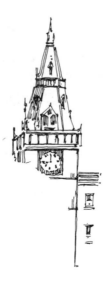

CAROL LAULA

Carol's song 'Standing Proud' won the competition for a song for Glasgow as European City of Culture in 1990. The beauty of her singing perhaps obscures the strength of her lyrics. She decided to write a song that would have an edge of criticism, not just be a puff of praise. She was surprised to win.

As always with overnight successes, Carol has been in the music business for ten years. Rather than sign with a big London company, she's with BURNONE, a new Glasgow label who are committed to Glasgow performers. Maybe the label will succeed then fade the way singing pubs and folk clubs have done, but that will be no failure.

Maybe success will pull Carol South to the big money and the big time contacts, but she is part of a tradition of Glasgow songwriters, and the next generation is hard on her heels.

Glasgow is hoatching with new bands and solo songwriters - the Glasgow Songwriters co-operative group has 40 members, writing songs across the folk and rock spectrum. As you pass any close, shout in 'Anybody up there write songs?' Wear a crash helmet - jeely pieces only make your hair sticky but cassettes make quite a dent in the skull.

STANDING PROUD

Carol has such a rich voice that I had never concentrated on the lyrics of 'Standing Proud'

She sang it on TV as the European City of Culture Year started, and was the best thing on that embarrassing item.

Then I met her, interviewed her for community radio, and asked could her song be used here. Still entranced by the sound, I sat to transcribe the lyrics.

And found myself moved by the imagery of the song, visualising a young man from one of our huge housing schemes, doing his best for his family and friends, hopeful for the future despite the pressing problems of here and now, proud and resilient but feeling the fragility of life.

And standing proudly, not bowed down by the weight of problems and centuries and other people's dirt.

In the hopeful climate of Europe just now it seems so apt that the song has been translated into and performed by Carol in Russian.

STANDING PROUD

He has a fam-i-ly and he has a home, he's wear-ing some new shoes that he does-n't quite own. He does-n't have work yet but he's trying hard to get. He'll give you his for-tune when he has one to give. And when it's o-ver and an-other year comes round, he'll tell all the stor-ies he learned and he'll leave us stan-ding proud. And he'll hold you- ou, he will hold you- ou, yes he'll hold you- ou with his charms.

Still has some dirt to wash from his clothes
It's been about a thousand years but some grass never grows
And don't you dismiss him and the pride in his eyes
He'll take all you give him but you won't break his spirit.

And when it's over and another year comes round
He'll tell all the stories he learned and he'll leave us standing proud
And he'll hold you, he will hold you
Yes, he'll hold you with his charms.

Words and music by Carol Laula
Published by Zomba Music

JIM MCKENNA

A 'floor singer'. One of the many you hear now and then in folk clubs. Floor singers don't get paid for singing, only the guest gets a fee. The floor singer does it for the love of the song, the glory and the experience. Some floor singers hope they'll eventually get paid as guest performers. Some, like Jim, don't wish for the big time.

Jim writes good songs, often along with someone else in the middle of a 'session' lasting a few hours. Then he'll sing them a few times, until they are overtaken by other songs and other priorities in his life.

'Songwriting is a pastime with me. Other people come along with an idea, and I get involved in turning it into a song.' If Jim performed in a semi-professional group his songs would get recorded—they are of professional quality.

How many thousands of good songs have been written, sung a few times, then lain in a drawer somewhere? This is not a sad story—Jim doesn't write his songs to get them recorded or try to get fame and fortune. He writes them because he has to—they demand to be written, then he like me and countless others feels some responsibility to the song, to give it an airing.

GEORGE SMITH

Jim sent me the following.

'A note on the co-writer George Smith. A shift worker for many years, first at Bathgate till the shutdown, now working 'Continentals' at Clydesdale.

'George's hobbies are music and boys' football. He has a son and daughter.'

SCREW'S BARLINNIE BLUES

'George Smith and I were sitting on top of the roof of my house. The things we were doing, the way a girl going by called up to us, made us both think of the rooftop protests in Barlinnie.

'George came round a couple of days later with the song idea, and we put it together. I've sung it six or seven times in public - now I'm sick of it. I'm a floor singer, I should do new songs—people quickly get fed up if you keep doing the same songs.' This song is scurrilous or honest—it depends on your point of view.

Are you up on the roof, down in the yard, outside peering in? This is Jim's and George's viewpoint.

SCREW'S BARLINNIE BLUES

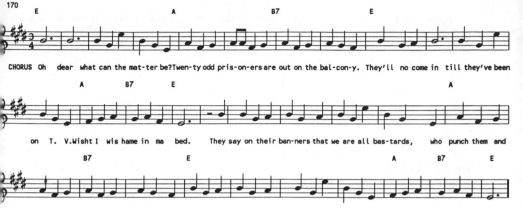

CHORUS Oh dear what can the mat-ter be? Twen-ty odd pris-on-ers are out on the bal-con-y. They'll no come in till they've been on T. V. Wisht I wis hame in ma bed. They say on their ban-ners that we are all bas-tards, who punch them and kick them and pee in their cus-tard. When we get back in there we'll feed them on mus-tard, I wisht I wis hame in my bed.

Now there's thon wee man out of cell number seven.
He's up on the rooftop, he thinks he's in Heaven.
When we get the bugger he'll be sorry he's livin'.
Oh I wisht I wis hame in ma bed.

A wee Glesga woman came pushin her pram.
Roarin and screamin up at a masked man.
'Hey Ronnie ya eedgit come doon when you can
So's I can go hame to ma bed.'

But Ronnie was roarin back down tae his wife,
'Get hame to your mother and get on with your ain life,
Big Slasher's up here and he's wieldin a big knife
So I wisht I wis back in ma cell.'

Now they've been on the telly and they've spoke on the News,
And the whole of the nation's been hearing their views
On how Big Sammy Ralston got done for wi the screws.
Oh I wisht I wis hame in ma bed.

Ah but haud on a minute I've just had the sign
That the warders frae B hall are gaun on double time,
Well I hope they stay up there, this'll juist suit me fine.
Oh I'm gled I'm no hame in ma bed.

Words by Jim McKenna and George Brown
Music 'Three Old Ladies'

23

ARCHIE FISHER

Archie Fisher, the patriarchal figure of the singing Fisher family, but really just the big brother of all those powerful singing women, originally became famous on STV as half of Rayanarchie, with his sister Ray. (See the song 'Shift And Spin'.)Now Archie is the presenter of Travelling Folk, BBC Radio Scotland's flagship folk music programme. As Director of Edinburgh International Folk Festival he steered it into the company of the biggest folk festivals in Britain. He is a freelance broadcaster, a record producer, an instrument maker and repairer. Oh, and he's a singer.

The original guitar stylist of the Glasgow scene, although he started on banjo, Archie first met Hamish Imlach in the playground of Hyndland School. Hamish came up and said 'Hullo, do you want to buy a cigarette lighter?'

Archie has over the years developed the richness and warmth of his voice, and has collaborated amongst others with Alan Barty, Barbara Dickson and Rab Noakes of Fife, Mike Heron and Robin Williamson of the Incredible String Band, Garnet Rogers of Canada, and Liam Clancy and the late Tommy Makem of Ireland.

As a song stylist he has breathed new life into many old Scottish songs, and supported new Scots songwriters. He even used to sing a song of mine called 'Dear Evelyn'. He did it proud.

THE SHIPYARD APPRENTICE

Archie has himself written and recorded many fine songs—'Men Of Worth', 'The Final Trawl', 'The Witch Of The Westmorelands', 'The Mountain Rain', and 'Lindsay The Fiddler'.

'The Shipyard Apprentice', also known as 'Fairfield Crane', is the most enduring.

It was written for a BBC radio series called *Landmarks*, the lyrics as a joint production with Norman Buchan, with a tune by Glasgow fiddler and Broomhill Bum Bobby Campbell. None of Norman's verses for the programme have been kept in Archie's sung version.

As the fortunes of the Clyde shipyards have changed over the years other hands have wanted to change the song. Alasdair Robertson and John McCreadie have both made amended versions.

THE SHIPYARD APPRENTICE

I was born in the shad-ow of a Fair-field crane, and the blast of a freigh-ter's horn was the ve-ry first sound that reached my ears on the morn-ing I was born I lay and I list-ened to the ship-yard noise com-ing out of the great un-known and was sung to sleep by the mo-ther tongue that was to be my own

But before I grew to one year old
I heard the sirens scream
As a city watched in the blacked out night
A wandering searchlight beam.
And then at last I woke and rose
To my first day of peace,
But I knew the battle to stay alive
Was never going to cease.

For I've sat and I've listened to my father tell
Of the days that he once knew
When you either sweated for a measly wage
Or you joined the parish queue.
And as times grew harder day by day
Along the riverside
I oftimes heard my mother say
'It was tears that made the Clyde.'

I've sat in the school from nine to four.
And I've dreamed of the world outside
Where the riveter and the plater watch
Their ships slip to the Clyde.
I've served my time behind shipyard gates
And I sometimes mourn my lot
But if any man tries to mess me about
I'll fight as my father fought.

Words by Archie Fisher
Music by Bobby Campbell
Published by Kettle Music

CILLA FISHER

Cilla, the youngest of this generation of the singing Fisher Family performs in a duo with her husband Artie Trezise.

They are impressive performers of traditional songs, with several fine albums, but that is all overshadowed by their mega status as Aunty Cilla and Uncle Artie of the Singing Kettle Show, the best children's show in Scotland bar none. The title arose because they live in Kingskettle, Fife.

They've released six albums of Scots kids' songs old and new, with a backing group of kids and ace instrumentalist Gary Coupland. The live shows are wonderful experiences of controlled pandemonium, with props that include a technicolour array of kettles. Except when they took the show to New Zealand, couldn't find any kettles, and had to do the Singing Teacup Show!

Norman Buchan recently, in a House of Commons debate on broadcasting and censorship, quoted a song he had collected from Cilla as a wee one.

> Mrs McGuire peed in the fire.
> The fire was too hot, she peed in the pot.
> The pot was too wide, she peed in the Clyde.
> And all the wee fishes ran up her backside.
> (Or 'And all the wee fishes turned over and died.')

This piece of honest vulgarity has of course no place in polite society.

CANNY SHOVE YER GRANNIE

The one song guaranteed to get any audience of any age singing. I learned recently that this is the 'party piece' of the Queen Mother, who is after all Scots.

It is puzzling that a cowboy song—'She'll Be Coming Round The Mountain When She Comes' - has been so firmly grasped in Glasgow and used by children. Perhaps the nonsense element of the verses helped - 'She'll be wearing pink pyjamas', 'She'll be riding six white horses'.

Perhaps the unspecific nature helps—who is this she who will come? Is it the all-powerful grannie, or Supermaw? As usual there are less attractive verses—sectarian or suggestive. I myself appropriated a friend's aphorism 'Never shove yer grannie when she's shavin' to make a verse which Nancy Dangerfield won't let me print here.

YE CANNY SHOVE YER GRANNIE

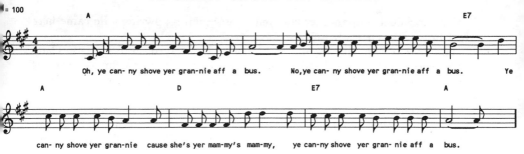

Oh, ye can-ny shove yer gran-nie aff a bus. No, ye can-ny shove yer gran-nie aff a bus. Ye can-ny shove yer gran-nie cause she's yer mam-my's mam-my, ye can-ny shove yer gran-nie aff a bus.

Ye can shove yer other grannie aff a bus. x2
You can shove yer other grannie cause she's just yer daddy's mammy.
Shove yer other grannie aff the bus.

Ah'm no Hairy Mary, ah'm yer maw. x2
Ah'm no Hairy Mary, ah'm yer maw's canary,
Ah'm no Hairy Mary, ah'm yer maw.

CHORUS
Singin I will if you will, so will I. x2
I will if you will, I will if you will.
I will if you will, so will I.

It's murder, mighty murder in the hoose.
When the cat he does the rhumba wi the moose.
If ye hit im wi a poker, he'll dae the Carioca.
It's murder, mighty murder in the hoose.

It's murder, mighty murder in the school.
It's murder, mighty murder in the school.
If ye canny dae yer spellin, they'll melt ye wi a melon,*
(OR : If you canny dae yer grammer, they'll hit ye wi a hammer)
It's murder, mighty murder in the school.

It's murder, mighty murder in the jail.
Where they feed ye breid and watter frae a pail.
If you ask them fur a tinny, they'll send ye tae Barlinnie,
It's murder, mighty murder in the jail.
    (* see glossary re 'mellin'.)

Music 'She'll Be Coming Round The Mountain'

27

ALASDAIR ROBERTSON

Alasdair Robertson, another adopted Glaswegian songwriter—he came here when he was seven.

Alasdair has five albums under his belt. He played at first with Cado Belle—a folk rock band ahead of its time—went to London for a couple of years. Came back and with Ken Campbell and Chris Miller formed the Ideal Band.

In between other projects he backed poet Liz Lochhead on keyboards for a 45 rpm disc called 'Men Talk'. Then came the Zydeco Ceilidh Band, an exciting mixture of Louisiana Cajun stomps and Scottish Country dance sounds.

Now Alasdair has emerged as a soloist. His latest album, *Friends and Companions*, shows his commitment to comment, with titles like 'Ballad Of A Young Anarchist' and 'The Rising', plus a reworking of the story of the terrible mine explosion in the mine at High Blantyre that the traditional song 'The Blantyre Explosion' commemorates.

Alasdair also wrote a much quoted 'Song For Glasgow'—you'll find it later in this book beside the tune it was set to, the old ballad 'Jamie Raeburn'.

KELVINGROVE

Alasdair has lived in Glasgow's West End many years, and used the green lung of the city's most dramatic and atmospheric park, Kelvingrove.

He says his song was written on his return from London, as a symbol of lifelong commitment to Glasgow. It's a song he is pleased with, as a good example of the craft of songwriting.

Kelvingrove Park has however also been responsible for song assassination.

There's a great old song, 'The Shearin's No For You', with fine lines like 'Take the buckles frae yer shoon, for yer dancin days are done.' The tune was hijacked for a prime sample of kailyard kitsch with verses the like of

> Let us haste to Kelvin Grove, bonnie lassie, o.
> Through its mazes let us rove, bonnie lassie, o.
> Where the roses in their pride deck the bonnie dingle side.
> Where the midnight fairies glide, bonnie lassie, o.

KELVINGROVE

In summer's warm attractions
as all the flowers unfold
we'll find our direction
watch the river flow;
and I'll see every change arrive
with you, my only love
as we take the winding paths of life
as we walk in Kelvingrove.

Then autumn winds come drifting
with a fragrance of their own;
that's the time for harvesting
our dreams will be full-grown.
And I'll see every change arrive
with you, my only love
as we take the winding paths of life
as we walk in Kelvingrove.

And then the migrant birds will go
there's winter in the trees;
the showers of spring have turned to snow
as dreams to memories.
And I'll see every change arrive
with you, my only love
as we take the winding paths of life
as we walk in Kelvingrove.

Words and music by Alasdair Robertson

29

ARTHUR JOHNSTONE

Arthur's latest album, *North By North*, on Lapwing Records, tells you simply 'Arthur Johnstone comes from Glasgow'.

There's more to him than that, of course. The songs span the USA, Ireland and England, with the strongest clutch being fine new Scots songs— plus a well-loved 'Benny Lynch', Matt McGinn's praise song for a boxing son of Glasgow.

The subjects? The struggles to get and keep work, the senseless struggles of war, and a couple of love songs.

Arthur, a man who loves a fine song, is clear about his priorities, and supports the struggle. When he lifts his voice, the noisiest pub will hush and the most footsore marchers get some new heart.

Though still fondly recalled as a member of a band of musical reprobates called The Laggan who supported the Folk Revival manfully, Arthur has built a new reputation as a solo singer at trades union rallies, Mayday meetings, and of course as the begetter and solid support of the Star Club, where he is fierce in defence of his music. Try chattering during a song and you'll discover.

THE JOHN MACLEAN MARCH

Written in 1948 by Hamish Henderson, Perthshire man now living in Edinburgh, fine poet and composer of extra-fine songs. (See 'The Freedom Come-all-ye'.) With Morris Blythman and Norman Buchan Hamish is a key figure of the Scottish folk revival.

In addition to his writing, Hamish found and recorded the songs of Jeannie Robertson, Jimmy McBeath and many other fine bearers of the tradition. A lovely man, generous with praise and support for performers and writers.

'This song was specially written for and sung at the John MacLean Memorial Meeting in St Andrew's Hall in Glasgow, 1948, at the twenty-fifth commemoration of the death of John MacLean. The singer was William Noble. The tune is traditional and has been arranged by the poet.' From *Homage To John MacLean*. The tune is a 'piper's version' of the old tune used for 'Scotland The Brave'.

This song has been called 'the first swallow of the Folk Revival'.

It was most recently recorded in exciting electro-funk form by the Glasgow group Tonight At Noon on the album *Down To The Devils*.

THE JOHN MACLEAN MARCH

Hey Mac, did ye see him as ye cam' doon by Gor-gie, A-wa ower the Lam-mer-law or
jin-ers and hau-ders-on are march-in' frae Clyde-bank; Come on noo an' hear him - he'll be
north o' the Tay? Yon man is com-in', and the haill toon is turn-in'oot. We're a' shair he'll win back tae
ower thrang tae byde. Turn oot, Jock and Jim-my: leave yer crans and yer muck-le gan-tries. Great John Mac-Lean's com-in'
Gles- gie the day. The
back tae the Clyde. Great John Mac-Lean's com-in' back tae the Clyde.

Argyle Street and London Road's the route that we're marchin'
The lads frae the Broomielaw are here—tae a man!
Hi Neil, whaur's your hadarums, ye big Heilan teuchter?
Get yer pipes, mate, an' march at the heid o' the clan.
Hullo Pat Malone: sure I knew ye'd be here so:
The red and the green, lad, we'll wear side by side.
Gorbals is his the day, and Glesgie belangs tae him.
Ay, Great John MacLean's comin' hame tae the Clyde.
Great John MacLean's comin' hame tae the Clyde.

Forward tae Glesgie Green we'll march in guid order:
Wull grips his banner weel (that boy isna blate).
Ay there, man, that's Johnnie noo—that's him there, the bonnie fechter.
Lenin's his fiere, lad, an' Liebknecht's his mate.
Tak tent when he's speakin', for they'll mind whit he said here
In Glesgie, oor city—an the haill warld beside.
Och hey, lad, the scarlet's bonnie : here's tae ye, Hieland Shony!
Oor John MacLean has come hame tae the Clyde.
Oor John MacLean has come hame tae the Clyde.

Aweel, when it's feenished, I'm awa back tae Springburn.
Come hame tae yer tea, John, we'll sune hae ye fed.
It's hard work the speakin'; och, I'm shair he'll be tired the nicht.
I'll sleep on the flair, Mac, and gie John the bed.
The haill city's quiet noo: it kens that he's restin'
At hame wi' his Glesgie freens, their fame and their pride!
The red will be worn my lads, an' Scotland will march again.
Noo Great John MacLean has come hame tae the Clyde.
Great John MacLean has come hame tae the Clyde.

Words by Hamish Henderson

31

IAIN INGRAM

Alison Duncan, who is a fine singer based in Dunoon, made a special trip to Glasgow to sing a song of Iain's in a song competition.

> Cauld winter's here again, come are days when many suffer
> In damp and draughty hames, on the road doon in the gutter.
> A time when those wi troubled lives, through hardship and despair
> Need a helping hand frae their fellow man tae greet the spring once mair.

Alison told me that 'Annie McKelvie', which I had been seeking for this book, was Iain's composition.

Alison told me that 'Annie McKelvie', which I had been seeking for this book, was Iain's composition.

Alison then sent me a tape of 'Annie', remarking 'Based on Iain's personal experience, but transposed to his favourite Edwardian era when he sings it!' There were another twenty songs on the cassette, which Alison had labelled 'Some of the songs of Iain Ingram'.

scrap of paper or cigarette packet, at any time day or night and wherever I happen to be. This is only done after a mental picture has been constructed.

'The subject matter is endless. Fictional tales, memories, historical fact, all mixed together with the music that has influenced me over the last 41 years.

'Before I proceed much further with the lyrics I start work on the music. Words and music are formed together in the first verse. The completed tale or scenario is firmly entrenched in my mind and the remaining verses and chorus (if any) follow fairly quickly.

'Ensuing days and sometimes weeks are spent trimming and polishing, chopping and changing the lyrics, altering certain notes, singing the song over and over till I'm satisfied I can do no more with it.'

ANNIE MCKELVIE

I heard this song first from one of the performers at a Women's Concert in Edinburgh. It seemed so totally convincing in its 1930s setting, I assumed it was old, and began to construct a story for myself of why it should have survived in the tradition, and why I'd never heard it before.

Iain has a rare ability—few songwriters can inject a convincing period feel into songs.

ANNIE MCKELVIE

Dumbarton's the place where I met Ann McKelvie, oot walkin alang the Clyde shore.

Oh, we blethered a while till as evenin was fallin we walked the road back tae her door. CHORUS Dae ye

fancy a night at the dancin wi me? The band in the Toon Hall's the finest ye'll see And if

there's no another place you'd raither be, then come tae the dance wi me, Annie.

She said 'Ah'd like a few days tae think ower yir proposal.
My mither wid hiv tae consent.'
So we parted that night wae a kiss on her doorstep
Then back hame through Bowling ah went.

Oh she finally agreed tae come oot wae me dancing
And travel tae Clydebank by train.
On that cauld station platform for hours ah waited
But never seen Annie again.

Noo it's oftimes ah've walked by the banks o the Leven
And followed her flow tae the Clyde,
And hiv thought o ma day spent wae Annie McKelvie,
The lassie that wounded ma pride.

Words and music by Iain Ingram
Published by Isa Music

33

'I've sung this song, and I'll sing it again'

The Glasgow Folk Club in The Corner House, Trongate

Adam McNaughtan—THE GLASGOW THAT I
USED TO KNOW
Alastair McDonald—SAM THE SKULL
Matt McGinn—ROB ROY MACGREEGOR-O
Hamish Imlach—COD LIVER OIL AND THE
ORANGE JUICE
Norman Buchan—AUCHENGEICH DISASTER
Enoch Kent—THE BLEACHER LASS O
KELVINHAUGH
Jimmy McBeath—ROVING BAKER FRAE
MULGUY

'I'VE SUNG THIS SONG, AND I'LL SING IT AGAIN'

In 1959 Norman and Janey Buchan felt there could be a folk club in Glasgow.

There had already been two or three visits from London-based performers like Ewan MacColl and Ralph Rinzler to perform in Ballads And Blues evenings upstairs in the Iona Community building in Clyde Street. These were exciting mixter maxter affairs, with Rinzler showing Archie Fisher banjo licks out on the stairs, Josh McRae being cheered on by the partisan local audience against visiting disapproval of his cowboy North East twang, and jam sessions combining Archie with Joe Gordon.

Then there was a concert featuring Josh White, black American singer of blues, ballads and distinctly odd versions of ditties like 'The Lass With The Delicate Air'.

Josh rather misjudged the audience and used his cabaret-style mannerisms of dedicating 'this next song to all the little children in the audience'. He also did his famous trick of tuning a guitar string so high it 'accidentally' broke, so he could change a string and sing a song at the same time. This as always brought the house down.

To our astonishment local boys Robin Hall and Jimmie Macgregor were appearing on national evening BBC TV, alongside fellow Scots Rory and Alex McEwan.

At the same time the Glasgow group The Reivers were singing Scots traditional songs on STV's Jigtime.

Moyna Flanigan, Rena Swankey, Enoch Kent and Josh McRae had been solo singers, all enthusiasts for the songs, who often appeared on the same platform. It was Norman Buchan who brought the Reivers together on the model of the American singing group the Weavers, especially to appear on Jigtime.

Moyna recalls that 'Josh was at the time doing his National Service down in Cairnryan. He was allowed off at the weekends, so he was able to hitch up on a Friday night to appear on TV. But he could not make the Thursday rehearsals with us—Enoch would say 'Josh is singing the next verse' and the camera would focus on an empty straw bale for a while.'

The Reivers sang traditional Scots songs, ranging from 'Mormond Braes' and 'Bonny George Campbell' to 'Rothesay-o' and 'Hot Asphalt'. 'We wanted to sing 'Black Is The Colour', but STV said it wasn't Scottish—so we quoted the verse about 'I go to the Clyde and I mourn and weep'. That convinced them.'

The Reivers had much success in the late 50s, making recordings, appearing in concerts, performing for the intervals at barn dances, and even touring dance halls in Scotland.

Younger singers in Glasgow were busy performing wherever they could corral an audience—social clubs, talent competitions, bingo halls and especially clubs for the elderly. The ever-tolerant old people of Glasgow have nurtured many a faltering talent, and some non-talents which might have been better throttled on sight.

Norrie and Janey thought it was time a club was started and run by young enthusiasts, so they asked various singers they knew to gather in their house.

The idea seemed a good one, although frankly we'd little idea of what was involved or what a folk club would look like.

A committee was formed, a meeting or two held, enquiries made and premises sought. I remember looking at an amazingly tatty coffee bar place in the West End, peeling black paint and dusty black curtains—I expected to find a dead bat at the bottom of my Coke.

By the end of summer only myself and Drew Moyes were left of the committee. Then Janey came up with a possible venue. A large lunchtime eatery called The Corner House, formica and metal, on the Trongate just two corners away from Glasgow Cross. The pleasantly pickled manager was quite tickled by the idea of an evening event.

He would charge a rent of five pounds for the evening, and hope people would eat a lot of sandwiches. Drew and I reckoned that we could just about stump up the fiver between us if no-one at all came on the night.

They came in herds. I almost wept with relief.

There was a drawback or two. Every time a tram rattled past whoever was singing had to stop 'until the noise has subsisted' as Willy McCulloch put it. Rescue came with some guys—I never learned their names—who after a few weeks began to bring in a mysterious set-up of microphone, wires and boxes which I learned was called a P. A.

There was already a folk club in Scotland—we made exchange visits with it. Hamish Henderson had encouraged some Edinburgh University students to get a University grant and set up a club.

But the Glasgow Folk Song Club was the first to operate as a self-supporting weekly club.

A few weeks more and we had our first guest—Jimmy McBeath was coming to sing in Edinburgh, and Hamish Henderson asked if the Glasgow club would like to book him.

BEAUTIFUL
BUTE

37

Regular performers at the Glasgow club were the Broomhill Bums, a ramshackle assembly of hedonists who were participating in the 19 month long party cum ceilidh in Hamish Imlach's house in Broomhill.

Those involved included Jacky O'Conner, Bobby Campbell, Archie Fisher, Ray Fisher, Hamish Imlach, Josh McRae, Sheila McRae, myself and others.

The emphasis was on the pleasure of singing, and to begin with our taste was for American music. We experimented with different styles, studying the sounds of banjo-assaulters like Aunt Samantha Bumgarner or Buell Kazee, the blues shouter Sonny Terry, the urban cowboy Rambling Jack Elliot. It depended what could be acquired on record. When we sang the Scots songs we sounded American.

We appointed ourselves experts. When the bluegrass banjo fire of Earl Scruggs first appeared—courtesy of bootleg pressings made in the Gallowgate and sold at the Barras—it was solemnly agreed that this was a technical speeded up fake, since the banjo could not physically be played at that speed.

We began to make connections with performers elsewhere. Martin Carthy, now a pillar of the English folk scene, turned up in Glasgow as the assistant stage manager of the touring company of *The Merry Widow*, and he and Archie Fisher traded guitar secrets.

At the time there were no teachers or printed tutors on acoustic guitar playing—you stumbled along and puzzled out what you could. You sat at the feet of visiting performers, trying to memorise their hand movements so you could attempt later to reconstruct. The knowledge we took years to acquire is now sooked up and digested in weeks by youngsters—it's no fair, so it's no. The flavour of the times is caught in Hamish's memory of the first time he was paid to sing in Aberdeen.

'The fee was ten pounds. A whole crowd came along from Glasgow including Archie, his mother Mrs Fisher, Gordon McCulloch and a guy called Charlie Yoga. He was an Indian from Zanzibar who played a classical Japanese instrument called the mini-tashkoto while he sang Gaelic songs. The fee paid for a huge carryout and fish suppers all round.'

All the time, at breakneck speed we were learning songs, and finding new sources by tracing back from the performers we knew to the ones they had learned from.

Lonnie Donegan led us to his source for 'Rock Island Line', the astonishing Leadbelly, born Hudie Leadbetter. A singer and 12-string guitar player of amazing power who had twice been imprisoned for murder. Both times he won early freedom by writing songs in praise of the State Governor—an interesting object lesson on the power of songwriting and the vanity of politicians.

Leadbelly sang black American chain gang work songs, blues, religious numbers and an eclectic mix of old popular numbers. (He even had one song in the 'pig latin' language of the ancient Roman Empire!)

Norman and Janie introduced us to the records of the Weavers, an American group including Pete Seeger who were active in the political struggles of the USA, leading to blacklisting through the UnAmerican Activities Committee of Joe McCarthy.

The Weavers in turn showed us the songs of Woody Guthrie. His *Dust Bowl Ballads* chronicled the hardships endured by migrant workers in the American Midwest in the 1930s. They had been farmers who lost their land to the anger of Mother Nature in huge dust storms that blew the fertile topsoil of their fields away—Steinbeck's *Grapes Of Wrath* tells the same story.

> I've sung this song and I'll sing it again.
> Honey, so long, it's been good to know you.
> This dusty old dust is a-gettin my home.

It's interesting to note how many of the Broomhill Bums drifted from home into a nomadic life-style. Another example of the power of song?

Although we were enraptured by the romance of the USA, we already sang and gradually placed more emphasis upon the songs of our own country.

At first these were learned from the recordings of Ewan MacColl and A L Lloyd, and of Jeannie Robertson whose 'Twa Recruitin Sergeants' and 'When I Was New But Sweet Sixteen' were early favourites.

We sang Glasgow kids' songs.

> Samson wis a mighty man, he faucht wi cuddies' jaws.
> He won a score o battles wearin crimson flannel drawers.
> Caesar wis a general, he thocht he wis the boss,
> But his legionnaires got cut tae bits when they focht at Brigton Cross.
> On the Royal Tour o Glasgow ye should have seen the Queen
> She wis playin a game o football wi the lads on Glasgow Green.
> The captain o the ither side wis scorin in fine style,
> So the Queen called ower a polisman and clapped him in the jile.

39

We sang 'The Calton Weaver', 'Frankie And Johnny', 'The Blantyre Explosion', 'The Barnyards Of Delgaty', 'John Henry', 'McPherson's Rant', 'The Bonny Lass Of Fyvie', 'Wild Mountain Thyme', and 'Goodnight Irene'. We sang Morris Blythman's songs.

> O, Scotland hasnae got a King, an she hasnae got a Queen,
> For ye canny hae the saicint Liz, when the first yin's never been.
> Nae Liz the Twa, nae Lillibet the Wan, nae Liz will ever dae:
> For we'll mak oor land republican in a Scottish breakaway.
> (To the tune of 'The Sash My Father Wore'.)

Our taste continued to widen. Music hall numbers grew in popularity—I remember a young man on vacation from University down south who came in and sang

> Oh, it's a braw bricht moonlicht nicht the nicht, och ee, och aye.
> The dew's among the heather and there's twa moons in the sky.
> There's Ronald, there's Donald, there's Willy, Jock and Tam.
> So dicht the clavers frae yer kilt and come and hae a dram.

I myself could sing every song so far recorded by Ewan MacColl so authentically that a rumour began that I had changed my name to be more like him. After all, Josh McRae had been Ian till he heard Josh White.

In fact, I was called Ewan before MacColl was, since I believe he changed his name from Jimmie Miller in 1945.

I also took liberties with the music that MacColl would not have countenanced. One of my specialities at the Corner House was to emerge from the little cashier's booth where I collected the admission money, cram my soft brimmed Humphrey Bogart hat down about my ears, and deliver a cod country song learned from a Peter Sellars album

> Come all ee young maidens, beware of the Fair.
> If ee on't know the way, then you'll find Oi right there.
> And the 'appiest toimes of me loife Oi dare say
> Oi've had showin young maidens the way.

In 1961 I went abroad. Drew Moyes moved the centre of operations from the Corner House to the Glasgow Folk Centre up a close in Montrose Street, and began to open other clubs in the West, so many he was nicknamed the Tsar of Folk Music. Other clubs like the Grand Hotel and Clive's Incredible Folk Club flourished.

By the time I came back to live in Glasgow in 1968 the folk scene had gone through several changes. On a 1964 visit everyone was singing Clancy Brothers choruses, while Bob Dylan simmered in the background. By 1968 comedy was taking over.

A song called 'Stewball' about a racehorse shows the sequence.

We learned it from Lonnie Donegan in a fast and furious version

> The old folk, uh-huh, they hollered, uh-huh.
> And the young folk, uh-huh, they bawled.
> And the children, uh-huh, cried 'Lord, Lord'
> At the noble Stewball.

Then Peter Paul and Mary taught us a sweet, sedate and rather silly version in which the horse 'never drank water, he always drank wine' and led the field by 'dancing and prancing'!

Enter Billy Connolly of the group The Humblebums. In 1968 the highly influential folk-life magazine *Chapbook* (never to be confused with the poetry magazine *Chapman*) published its collection of *SONGS FOR '68*. Among them was Adam McNaughtan's 'The Height Starvation Song', to become better known as 'The Jeely Piece Song'.

And a song by Billy Connolly to the Stewball tune and story.

> McGinty had a greyhound. It was called Caroline.
> And when she won races McGinty drank wine.
> He gave her devotion, and he took her for walks.
> Way up by Bellahouston and doon past the Docks.
> It would seem that he loved her, but it's no as you'd think.
> It's just the mair she won races the mair he could drink.

But Caroline is nobbled by a black pudding supper, McGinty goes to kick her but boots the electric hare and is 'instantly fried'.

Billy was right. The sickly sweetness that the Americans had brought into our music had to be doused in vinegar. More power to his elbow.

The Folk Revival veered away from solo singers towards groups, instrumental expertise and more exotic influences. Clubs were replaced by concerts and festivals. Now dancing is becoming more influential. Glasgow's professional folk performers get more work in Continental Europe or North America than at home. But the songs are still being written here.

41

ADAM MCNAUGHTAN

One of the Rutherglen Academy connection who were alerted to their country's songs by Norrie Buchan, Adam possesses a striking voice and appearance, and began early to write songs of strength and depth.

One evening in the basement of the Iona Community building where we met to try out and learn songs Adam showed me the lyrics of a song he'd just written about the clearing of tenements and the relocating of people in the new schemes out on the edge of Glasgow. Adam asked if I could think of a tune to put it to—I have always since regretted that I couldn't.

Adam found his own tune for 'Pullin Doon The Buildin Next Tae Oors', and never looked back.

He later wrote another song on the same theme—that favourite of adults who wish they were still kids - 'The Jeely Piece Song'. This song has a perhaps unique distinction - in Castlemilk a community centre has been named after it.

Adam's songs include trenchant social comment—his 'Blood On The Sand' asks the Scotland football squad how they can play on the bloodsoaked pitch of Chile's Santiago Stadium. 'We Will Not Have A Motorway' attacks plans to run a motorway through Glasgow Green.

One of Adam's finest is the lovely lyrical song, favourite of singers, 'The Yellow On The Broom', which derives from Betsy Whyte's book of this title about her childhood as one of Scotland's travelling people.

He is a singer of ballads, a member of the STRAMASH group, and an editor, writer, and collector of note.

THE GLASGOW THAT I USED TO KNOW

Adam sings his songs so well and distinctively it is hard to link any of them to other singers.

The principle of this book allows only one song against Adam's name, so it has to be 'The Glasgow That I Used To Know'.

This song was recently quoted to me as about Port Glasgow. I've seen it read out by Molly Weir on TV. It was read by Prince Charles when he opened Glasgow Garden Festival in 1988.

Adam's song has inspired at least two songs in answer, pointing out the harsher side of tenement living—'Caves In The Canyons' by Ian Davison, and 'Farewell To Glasgow' by Jim McLean, both printed elsewhere in this book.

THE GLASGOW THAT I USED TO KNOW

Oh, where is the Glas-gow where I used tae stey?
And where is the wee shop where I used to buy
The white wal- ly clos-es done up wi' pipe cley, where ye
a quar- ter o' tot-ties, a tup- pen-ny pie, a

knew eve-ry neigh- bour frae first floor tae third, and to keep your door locked was con-sid- ered ab- surd. Do
bag o' bro-ken bis- cuits an three tot- tie scones? and the wum- man aye asked, 'How's your maw get- tin' on?' Can your

you know the folk stey- in' next door to you?
big sup- er- mar- kets gie ser- vice like that?

And where is the wean that wance played in the street.
Wi' a jorrie, a peerie, a gird wi' a cleek?
Can he still cadge a hudgie or dreep aff a dyke?
Or is writin' on wa's noo the wan thing he likes?
Can he tell chickie-mellie fae hunch-cuddy-hunch?

And where is the fitba' that I played and saw,
The fair shou'der charge and the pass aff the wa'?
There was nae 4-3-3, there was nae 4-2-4,
And your mates didnae kiss ye whenever ye'd score.
Is the game, like big Woodburn, suspended sine die?

And where is the tramcar that wance did the ton
Up the Great Western Road on the old Yoker run?
The conductress aye knew how to deal wi' a nyaff.
'If ye're gaun then get oan, if ye're no then get aff!
Are there ony like her on the buses the day?

And where is the chip-shop that I knew sae well?
The wee corner cafe where they used to sell
Hot peas and brey and Macallums and pokes.
An ye knew they were tallies the minute they spoke:
'Dae ye wanta da raspberry ower yer ice-a-cream?'

Oh where is the Glasgow that I used to know?
Big Wullie, Wee Shooie, the steamie, the Co?
The shilpit wee bauchle, the glaikit big dreep,
The ba' on the slates, and yer gas in a peep?
If ye scrape the veneer aff, are these things still there?

Words by Adam McNaughtan
43

ALASTAIR MCDONALD

A well known performer, valued as a singer by the public, but precisely because of the kind of professionalism he exemplifies someone put down by the self-certificated experts of the folk fraternity.

Alastair has shown he can sing with the Scottish Radio Orchestra, play solo guitar, back up Gaelic singers, be a broadcast presenter, do cabaret and panto, play banjo in a trad jazz band.

No wonder he is suspect to purists in music who have problems doing one thing well.

Alastair has always sung politically committed material, like 'No Trident No' written by Alex Jamieson. It was also Alastair who made Alex's 'People's Palace' song well known.

Alastair has been around since the earliest days of the Scottish Folk Revival. On an album he did with Jim McLean Alastair recorded Jim's classic 'Massacre Of Glencoe'.

SAM THE SKULL

Various people told me this song must be in the book. Then I heard it on the Lismor album *THE PATTER*, an odd compilation which also includes two people conversing about Desperate Dan under the impression he is/was a Glaswegian.

Lismor didn't know the writer's name, but a local East End poet called Joe Dornan told me it was a friend of his called Harry Hagan.

The song was first recorded by Glasgow group Gaberlunzie, but it fitted so well into the type of songs about Glasgow furry or crawly creatures that Alastair is noted for, people kept asking in record shops for Alastair's (non-existent) recording of it.

I tracked Harry Hagan down.

'As a painter and decorator for Glasgow District Council—then the Corpy—I had on many occasions the chance to observe the local wildlife in some of Glasgow's toughest areas. One scheme, Barrowfield, was not at that time known for its genteel garden parties and afternoon teas!

'Working in this area I became conscious of the swashbuckling style of one particular cat. He feared nothing and no-one. In fact the dugs only came oot when he was at his tea! HE WAS SAM THE SKULL! The song wrote itself. Shettlestoon is poetic licence in place of Barrowfield.'

Harry was brought up in Carntyne, is married and has two grown up daughters, lives now in Baillieston and works as a 'fork-lift truck painter'.

SAM THE SKULL

♩= 100

CHORUS Ah'm a cat, ah'm a cat, ah'm a Gles-ca cat an ma name is Sam The Skull, ah've goat claws in ma paws like a
Ah roam a-roon doon in Shett-les-toon they aw know me by sight.' Here's the Skull, the Skull' you
where here's could

croc-o-dile's jaws an a heid like a fer-mer's bull. Ah'm no the kind a cat that sat oan the mat or the
hear them call as they dash in-tae the night. The po-lis stat-ion doon oor wey has

kind that ye gie a hug, ah'm the kind a cat that stran-gles the rats or ev-en the occ-as-ion-al dug.
baurs on the win-dae sull. They're no tae keep the prisoners in, they're keep oot Sam the Skull.
tae

There was a time no so lang ago, when they aw had had their fill.
And they sent for the RSPCA, tae come and catch the Skull.
There's naebody can get oot while he's roamin aboot.
Chasing aw the weans up the close,
Peein oan the stairs, scratchin his erse.
And sittin there picking his nose.

Oot came the men aboot hauf past ten in their wee blue Escort van.
Wan hid a sack wae a rifle oan his back, An wan hid a mallet in his hand.
Ah watched them run roon the side o the hoose
An ah casually strolled to the van,
Jumped in the front. I was off! Everything had gone tae plan.

Now you'll hear them say doon Shettlestoon way
'Whatever happened tae Sam the Skull?
He had claws in his paws like a crocodile's jaws
An a heid like a fermer's bull.'
Well you can tell them from me that ah'm still runnin free
And never a day is dull.
It may sound absurd, but ah'm living wae a burd
In a single-end in Maryhill !

Words and music by Harry Hagan
Published by Gaberlunzie Music

45

MATT MCGINN

In 1960 some singers would meet regularly in a room of the Iona Community building on Clyde Street to learn and try out new songs. It was an offshoot of Glasgow Folk Club. One night Janey came in with a guy even shorter than me—just back from being a student in the USA! He sang us a new song of his own to the tune of 'Tipperary'—'It's a long way to the Riviera, and to dear old Monaco'.

We were enchanted. As many and many an audience was soon to be. At a time when songwriters were as scarce as hens' teeth, Matt could spill new songs out at such a rate that many were off his performing list again before they could be put onto record.

'Red Yo Yo', 'Kirkcudbright Centipede', 'Three Nights And A Sunday', 'Coorie Doon', 'Can O Tea', 'We'll Have A Mayday', 'The Pill', and dozens more fine songs.

ROB ROY MACGREEGOR-O

This song of Matt McGinn's hits many targets squarely.

A chorus stuffed with the rich phrases that you hear and half understand, like 'Eat the breid' for an ever-hungry type. The admiring accusation 'The man that ate the biled ham raw' ranks alongside the burning question of 'Who stole the poultice aff the scabby-heidit wean?' And he ends with the apparently casual acceptance of violence in the home.

Then Matt mixes the language of kailyard politics 'Auld Scotia's wrongs' with the knuckle politics of the streets 'The leader of the Tong' and adds a casual tilt at the Royal Family.

The character of Highland rogue cum hero Rob Roy is changed into a giant mythological hero, the equal of Ireland's Finn McCool or Cuchulain, and like Glasgow's Rab Ha he has a gargantuan appetite.

Matt, the master songwriter, pokes fun at his own songwriting abilities, and reminds us that the spirit and gallusness of his delivery meant he could get away with silly or pointless verses at times.

I had hoped by the way to print at least five of Matt's songs in this book, but contractual problems arose. There's a fine collection of his work, with stories and autobiographical sketches, in *McGinn Of The Calton* published by Glasgow District Libraries. The Stramash group have made an excellent cassette of songs and extracts from the book, and issued it on the Greentrax label.

ROB ROY MACGREEGOR-O

On a dainty sandwich he's gey keen
Two loaves o' breid an' a pig between.

When tae the dancin' he has gane
He aye leaves fourteen lassies hame.

Who puts on size 15 shoes?
Drinks a barrel o' the rye-buck booze?

Who will right Auld Scotia's wrongs?
Who is the leader o' the Tongs?

He never ever sings a song
Unless it's a hundred verses long.

That wis a real wee rotten verse
This one here is ten times worse.

At London toon he had a look
Kiss'd the Queen and chased the Duke.

Frae Partick Cross up tae the Tron
Who knows every pub an' pawn?

Words by Matt McGinn
Music 'Duncan Gray'
Published by Heathside Music

HAMISH IMLACH

Another of the original gang of Glasgow folkies known as the Broomhill Bums. As Hamish Imlach himself says 'I was the only one of our age to have a house, so the party was at my place'.

Although he performs so seldom in Scotland that some journalists think he has retired, Hamish continues to sing and play up a storm across Europe.

I truly believe Hamish to be the best loved man on the folk scene. To be in his company is to be part of a movable party.

Fellow party members included then struggling youngsters like Billy Connolly and John Martyn. Hamish would take them along to his gigs, then pressure folk club organisers to let them play.

He is a blues stylist—a cross between Mississippi John Hurt and Brownie McGhee. He is noted for politically committed material—he was singing Hamish Henderson's compositions in the 60s, ten years before most singers came to them, and ended up on the black list of the Economic League as a Rooshan Red.

Hamish reserves his most inventive interpretive skills and pyrotechnics for comic songs.

COD LIVER OIL AND THE ORANGE JUICE

Hamish's undying contribution to this song is a patented evil laugh that in the words of one reviewer 'sounds like he gargles with razor blades'.

Hamish never expected 'Cod Liver Oil' to become the most requested song on British Forces Radio.

Although Hamish's version is so famous, I've followed the principle of this book and printed the original version, then called 'Hairy Mary'.

The song was written as a protest about overexposure to Hamish Imlach singing a beautiful number called 'Virgin Mary Had A Little Baby'. Carl MacDougall originated the song, then it passed through the hands of Ron Clark and Archie Fisher before reaching Hamish. When he recorded it he credited it to Carl and Ron as co-writers, but the then music publishers neglected to track them down. After all, Glasgow is a long way from London.

Then the publishers sold their stock of songs. When I started the GALLUS label I refused to pay royalties for the song away to the new publishers. On negotiation they agreed to pay back what they had, but most of its earnings were before their time. Carl and Ron got £27 each, a pound for every year of the song's life. Both Carl and Ron have handed their winnings on to good Scots political causes.

COD LIVER OIL AND THE ORANGE JUICE

Oot o the East there cam a hard man. A', A', a' the way frae Brig-ton.

CHORUS Oh, oh, Glo- ry Hal- le- lu-jah, Cod Liv-er Oil and the O- range Juice.

He went intae a pub an he cam oot paralytic.
Aw haw, V.P. an cider.

'Does this bus go tae the Denny Palais,
Aw haw, I'm lookin for a lumber.'

In the Palais he met Hairy Mary,
Aw haw, the flo'er o the Calton.

He says tae her : 'Hey hen are ye dancin?'
'Naw, naw, it's just the way ah'm staunin.'

He says tae her: 'Ye're wan in a million.'
'Aw, haw, so's yer chances.'

'Can I run ye hame, I've got a pair o sannies.'
'Aw haw, ye're helluva funny.'

Up the back close an doon the dunny
Naw, naw, it wasnae for the first time.

Her mammy came oot tae go tae the didgy.
Aw haw, he buggered off sharpish.

She tried tae find the hard man, He'd jined the Foreign Legion;
Aw haw, Sahara an the camels.

So Hairy Mary had a little baby.
Aw haw, its faither's in the Army.

Words by Carl MacDougall and Ron Clark
Music 'Virgin Mary Had A Little Baby' 1962
Published by Gallus Music

49

NORMAN BUCHAN

Norman Buchan, newly lost to us, was an MP, formerly Shadow Minister for the Arts, and earlier still English teacher at Rutherglen Academy. His work was crucial to the Glasgow Folk Revival.

Norrie had a weekly column in the Scotsman newspaper which was mandatory reading for singers in the late 1950s. Each week he gave a Scots folk song, with background. Bothy ballads, street songs, old ballads, new compositions.

These songs were lifted wholesale by recording artists, who then proceeded to claim the full copyright on the songs, even when Norrie had felt the song to be a little short and had therefore written an extra verse or two.

Youngsters at his school were taught about songs eg Ann Neilson, Gordeanna MacCulloch, Adam McNaughtan, Ian Davison.

A trail of youngsters, me among them, came to the Buchans' door in Partick to listen to records or copy songs from his book collection, and consult him about provenances.

He and his wife Janey, now an MEP, organised concerts of visiting performers which were sight unseen and curates' omelettes—I remember a West Indian Steel Drum Band which had only one steel drum, and an Irish Ceilidh Band who happily ignored the finer points of being in tune with each other. We were in those days delighted at any taste of the music that excited us.

His collection of *101 Scottish Songs* was the 'little red book' of the Scottish Revival. With Peter Hall Norman more recently edited an equally important collection, *The Scottish Folksinger*.

THE AUCHENGEICH DISASTER

Written at the time of the 1959 pit disaster at the pit, near Chryston.

Like some songs it was slow to be accepted, but it has been recorded on an album called *The Bonnie Pit Laddie* in 1975, and also by Five Hand Reel. It has won the accolade of authenticity, and been credited to Trad.

I had the moving experience of hearing it sung in the Auchengeich Miners' Welfare at a benefit concert during the 1984 Miners' Strike. The mine had been sealed off after the disaster, but the Welfare Club still serves the community.

THE AUCHENGEICH DISASTER

In Auch- en-geich there stands a pit, the wheel a- bove, it is- na turn-in.

For on a grey Sep- tem- ber morn The flames of Hell be-low were burn-in.

Though in below the coal lay rich
It's richer noo, for aw that burnin'
For forty seven brave men are deid,
Tae wives an' sweetherts ne'er returnin'.

The seams are thick in Auchengeich.
The coal below is black an' glistening
But och, its cost is faur ower dear,
For human lives there is nae reckoning.

Oh, coal is black an' coal is red.
An' coal is rich beyond a treasure;
It's black wi' work an' red wi' blood
It's richness noo in lives we measure.

Oh, better though we'd never wrocht,
A thousand years o' work an' grievin'.
The coal is black like the mournin' shroud
The women left behind are weaving.

In Auchengeich there stands a pit,
The wheel above, it isna turnin'.
For on a grey September morn
The flames o' Hell below were burnin'.

Words by Norman Buchan
Music 'Skippin Barfit Thro The Heather'

ENOCH KENT

Enoch was a member of the Reivers, along with Rena Swankey, Moyna Flanigan and Josh McRae. Enoch is the brother of MEP Janey Buchan. He attended Glasgow School of Art along with Josh and Jimmie Macgregor.

At one point the Reivers did a short tour of dance halls in Scotland. To his astonishment Enoch, a good looking lad, was at the receiving end of screaming girl fans at a couple of venues.

Enoch had a particular strong warmth of voice, especially when he sang 'The Bleacher Lassie'.

When the Reivers stopped performing as a group he moved to London, and formed the group The Exiles with Bobby Campbell and Gordon McCulloch. Eventually he went on to Canada, and is writing fine songs like 'The Farm Auction' there.

THE BLEACHER LASSIE

In his classic collection of songs John Ord states 'The Bleacher Lassie appears to have been originally a Glasgow street song, but became a favourite all over the country.' This is of course a different use of the term 'street song' from the small children's gems we think of now. Jimmy McBeath was also a noted performer of this song—with actions!

I do not understand why the bleacher lassie didn't at least kick her returning boyfriend sharply in the shins when he had the cheek to test her faithfulness!

In fact, I've always suspected that the happy ending was tacked on by some sentimental singer who wanted 'tae make the lassie happy'. The final two verses do not fit the mood of the rest of the story.

One minute the storyteller seems genuinely heartsore. The next either he has just revealed himself to be her missing sailor boy, or her boyfriend has appeared from nowhere. At the very least a verse is missing.

And in fact in 1965 collector Pete Shepheard recorded the song at a berry camp near Alyth. The singer, a traveller called John MacDonald, calls his version 'the old way' of the song. He omits the last two verses altogether.

THE BLEACHER LASSIE O' KELVINHAUGH

As I was walk-ing one sum-mer's even-ing, a walk-ing doon by the Broom-ie-law,
It was there I met with a fair young maid-en. She'd cher-ry cheeks and a skin like snaw.

Says I 'My lass, is it you that wanders
All by yourself on the Broomielaw?'
'Oh, indeed, kind sir, I'm a bleacher lassie
In Cochrane's Bleachfields in Kelvinhaugh.'

Says I 'My lassie, will ye gang wi' me?
I'll dress ye up in fine satins braw.'
'Oh, no, kind sir, I may plainly tell you
I've a lad o' my ain, but he's far awa.'

'It's seven years that I lo'ed a sailor,
It's seven years since he's gane awa.
Ah, but seven times seven I'll wait upon him
And bleach my claithes here on Kelvinhaugh.'

Says I 'My lassie, you are hard-hearted.
I wish your fair face I never saw,
For my heart is bleeding baith night and morning
For the bleacher lassie o' Kelvinhaugh.'

'Oh, lassie, lassie, ye hae been faithful
And thocht on me when far awa.
Twa herts will surely be rewarded.
We'll part nae mair here on Kelvinhaugh.'

Now this couple they have got married,
And they keep an alehouse between them twa.
And the sailor laddies they all come drinking
To see that lassie on Kelvinhaugh.

JIMMY McBEATH

The very first paid guest at the Glasgow Folk Club. We paid him eight pounds, more money than he'd ever received for singing in his life. I was embarrassed at the degree of his gratitude.

Jimmy sang with an amazing North East rasp and tremendous vigour. Hamish Henderson first met him in an Elgin model lodging house in 1951. Jimmy was a street singer and a treasure house of Scots folklore.

He became a major influence on the Scottish Folk Revival. The fine range and quality of his songs reached from the bothy ballads of farm life like 'Nicky Tams' to old tales of heroic deaths like 'McPherson's Farewell'. He was especially effective on comic epics—'Sat And Grat For Gruel' or 'The Moss Of Borrowdale'.

THE ROVING BAKER FRAE MULGUY

I can't resist this song. It's an odd mixture of original lines, phrases lifted from other songs, and a tight rhyme scheme which the writer has to skip over now and then.

The notion of 'A rovin baker frae Mulguy' creases me—perhaps in those days baking was a swashbuckling trade!

I hadn't known that feeing took place on Glasgow Green. The Feeing Markets or Hiring Fairs took place twice a year in the Lowlands, in May and November, when farm or house servants could change their employment. They would gather in a public place—a market or in this case a park—to meet possible employers. Of course you wore your best working clothes, hence the lass's worry about the rain.

So the lass by missing her feeing time might not have a job for the next six months.

Or maybe Glasgow also had a Rascal Fair the Friday following the Feeing Market? At the Rascal Fair you'd find the servants who had found the new place not to their taste and had run off to try again.

In another version of the song the lass berates the baker by announcing she is her mother's sole support, then she agrees to marry the lad the next day!

Both communities have grown, so that Milngavie is now on the edge of Glasgow, not miles distant as when this song was written.

Milngavie is of course pronounced Mulguy—I don't know whavie.

There are many traditional and rewritten songs like this in the collection of thousands printed by The Poet's Box in Glasgow, and now held in the Glasgow Room of The Mitchell Library.

THE ROVING BAKER FRAE MULGUY

When drawing nigh I chanced to spy
A lassie walking by hersel.
For fear the rain her claes would stain
I shared wi her my umbrell.

'Oh, where are you going, my bonny lass?
Or are you bound far on this way?'
'To Glasgow toon, sir, I am bound.
For you know this is wir feeing day.'

I asked her if she'd take a dram,
Whisky, brandy, rum or wine?
She gave consent and in we went.
Into an alehouse by the way.

Glass after glass the rounds did pass
Till we both forgot it was feeing day.
Till the clock struck three, and she smiled on me
Saying 'Baker lad, the fault is thine.

(to second part of tune)
'The road is lang and I'm far frae hame.
And besides I've lost my feeing time.'

'Oh, cheer up, my lass, my bonny lass.
We'll get good weather by and by.
And don't be sad while wi a lad,
The rovin baker frae Mulguy.'

'Aa breenge in!'

The Blythman house in Balgrayhill, Springburn

Josh McRae—YURI GAGARIN
Morris Blythman—DING DONG DOLLAR
John MacEvoy—WEE MAGIC STANE
Jimmie Macgregor—PACK YOUR TOOLS AND GO
Nigel Denver—MAGGIE'S WADDIN
Andy Hunter—KILBOWIE HILL
Duncan Macrae—WEE COCK SPARRA

'AA BREENGE IN!'

In Scotland, and in Ireland, there used to be certain houses that were so conducive to good times and fine company of song and story they were called 'ceilidh houses'. People would travel miles on a dark and stormy night to get to them, and 'the crack would be mighty', with singing and story-telling, music and laughter.

In Balgrayhill Road, Springburn, Glasgow, there was a ceilidh house in the 1950s. The home of Morris and Marion Blythman, there you would find by invitation a company of rare quality.

On occasion there might be pipers—the Blythman's elder daughter Joanna was famed for her ability to sleep while six pipers tuned up in her bedroom.

But Balgrayhill Road was the kingdom of One Singer One Song. It was in the Blythman living room I first met and heard Jeannie Robertson, Jimmie Macgregor, Robin Hall, Josh McRae, Jim McLean. I was a player of the washboard at the time and able to sing every song ever recorded by Lonnie Donegan.

Jimmie, a professional then playing in a professional Skiffle group in London, advised me to play washboard in a less sophisticated manner, and enchanted us all with a new song he had just learned. It was called 'Day-oh', or 'The Banana Boat Song'.

> Come, Mr Tallyman, tally me bananas.
> Daylight come and me wanna go home.

Jeannie Robertson, the queen of traditional Scots singers, enthralled us with her 'big ballads' of lords and ladies in love or battle, tales of young men out on the town being tricked out of their wages by clever lassies, laments for lost loves and for new growing life that would chain those lassies to a cradle. And fragments of songs to set you wondering where the rest might be found.

> As I cam in by the Gariochland, an doon by Netherhaa.
> Forty thousand Hielandmen were merchin tae Harlaw.

> When I was new but sweet sixteen,
> And beauty just in bloomin, oh.
> It's little, little did I think
> That at nineteen I'd be greetin, oh.
> For the plooboy lads are gey braw lads
> But false and deceivin, oh.
> They'll tak aa, an they'll gan awa
> And they'll leave their lassie grievin, oh.

> We are three wee Glesca molls, we can let you see.
> And if ye hit the one wee moll ye'll hae tae hit the three.

58

Robin, a couple of years senior to me in school and about to seek the big time down south, showed us how those old songs could be sung by a young voice, and a guitar accompaniment added without doing violence to the feeling or the magic. His version of 'The Baron Of Brackley' was an Icelandic saga brought to life.

> Doon Deeside cam Invereye, whistlin and playin,
> And he was at Brackley's yetts e'er the day was dawin.
> And are ye there, Brackley, and are ye within?
> There's sharp swords are at yer yetts, will gar yer bleed spin.

When Robin joined forces with Jimmie Macgregor they took the traditional songs of Scotland to heights and places we could not have dreamed of. Their recordings were the major source for the new generation of singers to learn songs. The words could be found in Norman Buchan's book of *101 Scottish Songs*, but for the tunes and the feel of the songs youngsters went to Robin and Jimmie.

Their appearances on evening TV had for me the importance that some Scots attach to football. Each song was a goal scored against the pap pop music of the Hit Parade.

Jim McLean could weave a new topical song of biting wit out of the day's headlines. Yet Jim, unlike nearly all songwriters around or after that time, had no interest in performing for an adoring public.

> It was busy in the jungle, all the animals had came,
> To console their friend the tiger, who would soon be Royal game,
> But the tiger wasn't having it, he didn't think it fun
> To be stopping Royal bullets from Prince Philip's Royal gun.
> Yippi-i-ay! Yippi-i-o!
> Ghost tigers in the sky.
>
> Have you heard of Lady Chatterley?
> Sick and starved o love was she.
> Hey, hey, pair wee Lady Chat.
> Good Sir Clifford wis her man,
> He got shot in the war and he couldnae stand,
> Hey,hey, sad wee Lady Chat.

59

And Josh McRae took the American and Scots, the skiffle and blues and big ballads and kids' songs, and spun them into a web of affection and respect for the song—whatever its native home—that ensnared us all.

I missed the visits to Balgrayhill of Peggy Seeger, Alan Lomax, Lonnie Donegan, Flora McNeill of Barra—but I heard the tapes. Morris had a big powerful Grundig tape machine which recorded many historic performances. I wonder where those tapes are now?

The whole show was presided over by Morris. He got me and Nigel Denver and Andy Hunter and countless other kids to take an interest in our own traditional music by running a Ballad and Blues Club in Allan Glen's School, Glasgow—an establishment I attended for two years, along with Andy Hunter, who recorded some memories of those days.

'We called Morris the Moonman because he was so eccentric in his ways. He knew how to motivate and interest young people. Josh McRae, at that time a student at Glasgow Art School with Jimmie Macgregor and Enoch Kent, came to our school once a week to teach us guitar chords and songs. Josh showed us that you could switch from blues to Scottish traditional songs, and take an interest in both styles.

'Morris encouraged that. He wanted us to sing Irish Rebel songs, Orange songs, Scottish and American—he wanted us to see there was a world-wide fraternity of folk song.

'Eventually the club was virtually banned by a music teacher who didn't want to know about folk song. At this time Morris was away teaching in Turkey for a year. But the main work had been done.'

Remember that at this time practically the only place to hear these songs was in someone's house or in a Youth Hostel singsong. No records, no clubs, no concerts, only a very occasional radio broadcast.

In 1953 Ewan MacColl published a wonderful collection of songs under the title *Scotland Sings*, and included eight of the songs that are in this book. He and Hamish Henderson, Morris and Norman Buchan, with visiting firemen like Alan Lomax, made the Scottish Folk Revival by the way they encouraged, taught, and collected and disseminated songs. And wrote new songs.

Like MacColl and Henderson, Morris Blythman did not view song-writing as some arcane or specialised craft. He considered folk songs could be made by any member of the folk who cared to.

'Everyone in the world has one good song inside them,' he told me repeatedly. 'Some have more than one song waiting to come out, but everybody has one. Away and write your good song.'

I took Morris at his word and went off to write a song.

I was at the time much impressed by a record of army songs which had been put together by Ewan MacColl and A L Lloyd. And I was not looking forward with any pleasure to the prospect of being Nationally Served myself in the near future. I combined phrases and terminology from the songs with a couple of newspaper stories about the way National Service conscripts were mistreated, added some obscure historical references, and fitted it all to an American monologue cum song format I'd learned from the singing of Woody Guthrie.

> I was sittin with ma gittar, playin the blues,
> I heard the postman comin, he was bringin bad news.
> Got a letter, said 'Better get out of that civilian rut.
> There's a vacant bed a-waitin in an Army hut.'
> I didn't say much. I fainted.
> Early next morning I went off to catch my train.
> I said good-bye to mum and dad and Jane.
> Jane said she'd wait for me until Hell froze.
> Must have been a cold winter.

This mishmash, titled 'Talking Army Blues' and performed by Josh McRae, reached Number Six in the Hit Parade in 1959! The only chart it did not figure in was an obscure and unreliable trade publication. But this chart became more reliable later, and is used as the source for the big TOP TWENTY books of lists published by a famous brewer. So my song has been stricken from the record books—along with many others!

Having followed Morris's dictum and written my good song, I didn't try to write another song for seven years.

Andy Hunter had begun writing songs before me. His big hit at the time was 'Baron James McPhate', which explored the idiocies of the perennial Rangers and Celtic rivalry.

> James McPhate was a Glasgow lad, o fame that is faur and wide.
> He's kent frae auld Dumbarton tae the toon o East Kilbride.
> Jamie was a rovin boy, though civilised o late,
> For ye'll see him wheel his barra up and doon the Gallowgate.

Morris was an exceptional poet and songwriter himself. 'Aa breenge in!', the title of this chapter, comes from Morris's poem 'Til The Citie O John MacLean' in which he anticipates that the Glasgow of John MacLean's Red Clydeside will rise again and

> guide the warld
> Ti flourish.

He was criticised for using so many Orange tunes and references in his campaigning songs. Even when he co-wrote them with ex-Catholic Matt McGinn, as in 'Boomerang' to the tune of 'Bless Em All' when the chorus is in part

> We dinnae like gifts that go bang.
> Juist try wan an see if ah'm wrang.
> The banners are wavin: Wha's next for the shavin?
> So open the boom; boomerang!

For another example, Morris and the poet T. S. Law both worked on the song 'The Glesca Eskimos', which made use of the American Civil War tune 'Marching Through Georgia'. They were reclaiming the tune, which had been used in Glasgow for an Orange song, in which 'Hurrah, hurrah, we bring the Jubilee' became 'Hullo, hullo, we are the Billy Boys'.

This is the only example of a political tune I know—several people have been quite agitated at the idea of singing any lyrics at all to this tune in Glasgow, because of its association with Protestant extremism and anti-Catholicism.

> It's up the Clyde comes Lanin, a super-duper Yank,
> But doon a damn sight quicker, when we cowpt him doon the stank.
> Up tae the neck in sludge an sewage fairly stops yuir swank,
> We are the Glesca Eskimos.
> Hullo! Hullo! we are the Eskimos, Hullo! Hullo! the Glesca Eskimos.
> We'll gaff that nyaff caa'd Lanin, We'll spear him whaur he blows.
> We are the Glesca Eskimos.

Morris wrote 'I have always believed in mass creation. That is why I adopted the pen-name 'Thurso Berwick'. My hope was that other poets could be persuaded to write under this name which was chosen as the name of the people, those people from Thurso in the North to Berwick in the South. I did not realise then that poets do not like writing under any name other than their own.'

Nor do songwriters. So if you consult songbooks edited by Morris at the time—*The Rebel Ceilidh Song Book* is the best known—you'll find the songs are ascribed to individuals. The names chosen were based on who had contributed most to each song, from a 'workshop' which at times included Jim McLean, Jimmy Ross, Susan Haworth, Matt McGinn, John Mack, Alastair McDonald, Ian Wade, T S Law and others. (Jim McLean told me recently that many lines in both 'Glesca Eskimos' and 'Boomerang' are in fact his.)

The Blythman ceilidh house on Balgrayhill was the kingdom of One Singer One Song, but each song had to have something to say to the audience. None of your whingeing self-regarding teenage angst here. The songs of the people, but as Morris wrote 'not the prisoners of the tradition, if you like. We are rather the developers of the tradition.'

And the best songs were those with a chorus, so that audience and singer became one.

Someone might sing a 'traditional' assault on the unco good which fitted a Wee Free hymn tune and singing style to the following words.

> Joe Weevis was a wicked man, we'll see his like no more.
> He stole his father's coffin lid to make a hen-house door.
> The High High Notes of Martyrdom are unco hard to raise.
> And stretching hard to reach them gars the lassies burst their stays.

Morris might respond with a new assault of his own on the unco good which fitted the Welsh tune 'Cosher Bailey' to these words.

> Billy Graham came to Glasgow for to save us from damnation,
> And like Trigger and Roy Rogers he was welcomed at St Enoch's Station.
> Billy booked up the Kelvin Hall, man, ye should have seen his circus.
> It was bigger, it was better than the one that comes at Christmas.
> Billy then went on to Hampden, all the fans thought he was kiddin
> When they saw a great big notice sayin 'All sweiry words forbidden!'
> But Billy kept on winning, for we all felt good and trembly.
> Till the Devil got Stan Matthews to beat us 7-2 at Wembley.
> Billy knew the game was up, it was 'Farewell, Sauchiehall Street'.
> But he'll come again to Glasgow when he gets more funds from Wall Street.

JOSH MCRAE

Very well beloved. At his funeral in 1977 it was 'standing room only'.

The farewell oration was given by Jimmie Macgregor, who wrote in an Appreciation in the Scotsman newspaper.

'I spent my student years at the Glasgow School Of Art with Josh, and he was the first person I ever heard actually play the guitar. At that time he played blues very much in the style of the late Josh White, thus earning the name which stayed with him for the rest of his life.

'In my first year as a student, two people at the Art School played guitar. I was the other. When I graduated four years later, there were at least twenty.

'People still know the songs Josh made famous, and when Yuri Gagarin made the first space flight, Roddy McMillan's song, sung by Josh, went round a delighted world, and became a colossal hit in Russia.

'Josh McRae's contribution to the very earliest days of the folk music revival in this country cannot be overestimated. Josh had, in full measure, those qualities which I value most highly, and find so readily in my folk-singing friends, warmth and humanity.'

(Jimmie Macgregor)

Josh was special for all of us—he encouraged us to sing, showed us that a guitar could be a friend and support, but the song must be respected and its value teased out of it. His ability to combine American and Scots influences was an education for all of us.

Lonnie Donegan recorded a song called 'Talking Guitar Blues', an Ernest Tubbs number that Josh was famous for performing in Glasgow. Josh was to record a 'cover version', and asked for my 'Talking Army Blues' as a possible 'B side' song.

On release, the B side became the A side and the record became a hit.

Josh went on to make further singles and albums.

Ironically he is now best remembered for a novelty song—a Tony Hatch ditty called 'Messing About On The River'!

YURI GAGARIN

As Jimmie Macgregor says, Josh's singing of this song was a hit.

Josh went to an International Youth Festival in Moscow, and found that on every lamppost in the city centre was hung a loudspeaker, each one playing his recording.

YURI GAGARIN

CHORUS Oh dear, Yu-ri Ga-ga-rin, he flew tae the moon when it looked like a far-thing. He said tae the boys at the mo-ment of part-ing "Ah'm juist gaun a-way for the Fair". Now in-side the ship he lay down like a he-ro, the doors were sealed up and the count-down wis near-o, Ten-nine-eight, seven -six-five, four-three-two, one-ze-ro an Yu-ri went up in the air.

Now when he took off he wis shook tae the marra,
He circled the poles and he saw the Sahara,
He gave them a wave as he passed over Barra
The day he went up in the air.

Now when he went up it wis juist aboot dawning,
The time when the rest of the world wis still yawning.
Then Yuri returned tae the land he wis born in
Withoot even turning a hair.

When he came tae London they tried the saft pedal,
A wee bowler hat and a rolled-up umbreddle.
But the foundrymen went an they struck him a medal
An gied it tae him at the Fair.

Words by Roddy McMillan
Music 'Johnny's So Long At The Fair'

1961

65

C

MORRIS BLYTHMAN

For a Fifer Morris had an impressive way with Glesga speech patterns. He not only believed but proved that songs could be composed communally and then used for 'demonstration singing' to support and hearten people on marches and demos. At the same time the songs would enlighten onlookers as to the issues that were being raised.

His issues and topics for songs included general principles like Scots independence, Republicanism and Marxism—he was 'all out for a Scottish Workers Republic'—and specific struggles like the anti-Polaris movement, university rectorial elections, parliamentary byelections, and events like the reclaiming of the Stone Of Destiny in 1953 and the bombing campaign against ERII pillarboxes.

There is a cassette and booklet available of his songs and poems, issued jointly by the Gallus and Songs From Under The Bed labels.

Morris fitted the now generally known tune to the old ballad 'The Twa Corbies'. The tune belonged to an ancient Breton song called 'Al Alarc'h'.

I have tried earlier in this chapter to indicate how important Morris was to the Folk Revival. He edited a number of crucial small publications of songs, and persuaded people to write new songs for them—*The Rebel Ceilidh Song Books, Homage To John MacLean, Sangs O The Stane, Sangs Against the Bomb.*

The *DING DONG DOLLAR* album of 'Anti-Polaris and Scottish republican songs' issued on Folkways took the message of Scottish resistance to the USA.

Morris wrote in *Chapbook* magazine that 'The Scottish literary tradition is quite clear. You speak out for the people all the time. It is a people's  tradition, a radical tradition. Whoever or whatever happens to coincide with the people's tradition, be it CND, Sky-High Joe, the people who took the Stone of Destiny; you back them up and you don't split hairs.'

DING DONG DOLLAR

In view of Morris's belief in communal composition, I felt his song here should be one that he wrote jointly.

Glaswegian John Mack, also known as John Smith (Jak) heard George MacLeod of the Iona Community say 'You cannot spend a dollar when you are dead'. John Smith got the basic chorus idea, then he and Morris refined it and Jim McLean joined in the working up of the verses.

It became the anthem of the Scottish Anti-Polaris movement.

DING DONG DOLLAR

Oh, the Yank-ees they drappt an-chor in Dun- oon. They had a civ- ic wel-come frae the toon,

As they cam up the mea-sured mile Bon-ny Ma- ry o' Ar-gyll wis wear-in span-gled drawers her goon. be-low

CHORUS Oh, ye can-ny spend a dol-lar when ye're deid No, ye can-ny spend a dol-lar when ye're deid.

Sing-in Ding Dong Dol- lar, eve-ry bo-dy hol-ler Ye can-ny spend a dol-lar when ye're deid.

O, the Clyde is sure tae prosper noo they're here.
For they're chargin wan an tenpence for a beer.
Ay, an when they want a taxi,
They shove it up their—jersey
An charge them thirty bob tae Sandbank Pier.

An the publicans will aa be daein swell,
For its juist the thing that's shair tae ring the bell.
O, the dollars they will jingle,
They'll be no a lassie single,
Even though they mebbe blow us aa tae hell.

But the Glesca Moderator didnae mind,
In fact, he thinks the Yanks are awfy kind,
For if it's heaven that ye're goin,
It's a quicker wey than rowin
An there's shair tae be naebody left behind.

Words by Thurso Berwick and John Mack with Jim McLean
Tune 'Ye Canny Shove Yer Grannie'

JOHN MACEVOY

As far as I know this is the only song Johnny MacEvoy ever wrote. He went off to Canada in the late 1950s.

Morris Blythman wrote that when on Christmas Night 1950 the Stone was removed from Westminster Abbey and returned to Scotland.

'For the first time in generations Scotland had asserted herself in an active way. This was a departure from the passive whining about what England was doing to us and a real blow for freedom.

'Within days Scots were writing quite independently at all levels about this great event.'

Satirical song was used strongly. Morris himself flyted at the luckless Superintendent Barratt who led the hunt—

> There wis a wee super o Scotland Yaird
> Barraty-parraty, cocatou
> He cam up ti Glesca—He wisna feared
> Barraty-parraty, gie him ti charity
> Niver fund clarity, niver a clue.

When Morris led seven others to Central Station, Glasgow, to welcome with song a new batch of police searchers, the authorities feared a riot and diverted the train.

WEE MAGIC STANE

This most popular and enduring of the many Stane songs features the then Provost of Glasgow.

The mason who made the fake one which was returned to Westminster and still lies beneath the throne was also a Glasgow Councillor—Councillor Bertie Grey. He later presented to a church in Dundee a stone which he stated was the original he had copied.

This stone was on show in the People's Palace on Glasgow Green in 1990 as the real and original Palace of Westminster Stane.

(It is not of course the Stone Of Destiny on which the Kings of Scotland were formerly crowned. That stone was of black basalt, not the sandstone item featured in the song and under the throne in the Abbey. People believe that the original Stone was successfully hidden from the advancing English in 1296. It is still being sought. There's a rumour it is in Saudi Arabia.)

THE WEE MAGIC STANE

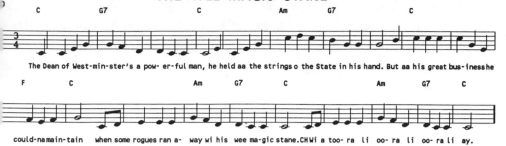

The Dean of West-min-ster's a pow-er-ful man, he held aa the strings o the State in his hand. But aa his great bus-iness he could-na main-tain when some rogues ran a- way wi his wee ma-gic stane. CHWi a too- ra li oo- ra li oo- ra li ay.

The Stane had great powers that could dae sic a thing
That withoot it it seemed we'd be wantin a King.
So he sent fur the polis and made this decree.
'Go hunt out the Stone and return it to me.'

So the polis went beetlin up tae the North
And they hunted the Clyde and they hunted the Forth.
But the wild folk up yonder just kidded them aa
For they didny believe it was magic at aa.

Noo the Provost o Glesga, Sir Victor by name.
Wis awfy pit oot when he heard o the Stane.
So he offered the statues that stand in George Square
That the High Church's masons might mak a few mair.

When the Dean of Westminster with this was acquaint
He sent for Sir Victor, and made him a saint.
'There's no use you sending your statues down heah,'
Said the Dean, 'But you've given me a jolly good ideah.'

So they quarried a stane o the very same stuff
And they dressed it all up till it looked like enough.
Then he sent for the Press and announced that the Stane
Had been found, and returned tae Westminster again.

When the reivers [theives] found out what Westminster had done
They went about digging up stanes by the ton,
And for each one they feenished they entered the claim
That this was the true and original Stane.

But the cream of the joke still remains tae be telt.
For the bloke that wis turnin them aff on the belt
At the peak o production was so sorely pressed.
That the real yin got bunged in alang wi the rest.

So if ever ye cam on a stane wi a ring
Just sit yerself doon and proclaim yerself King.
There's nane will be able tae challenge yer claim
That ye've crooned yerself King on the Destiny Stane.

Words by John McEvoy
Tune 'Villikens And His Dinah'

69

JIMMIE MACGREGOR

Jimmie first became famous as half of Robin & Jimmie. Now he is a radio presenter, a TV walker and talker, a tune composer and writer. 'All the elements of my life, my interests in wildlife, music, walking, history and writing—they're all pulling together now.'

When he and Robin Hall sang on the *TONIGHT* programme on BBC TV - five nights a week for four years—the folk songs we championed and loved were appearing there on the box! People we had met at school or at Balgrayhill were now professional singers!

Morris Blythman wrote for Jimmie a singing identity card to mark his reputation as an accompanist and harmony singer. He set it to the tune of 'The Means Test Man'.

> I'm no a Donegan or Duncan, a Ewan or Rory McEwen.
> By the time ye hear me play ma second bar
> There ye say, right away, it's Jimmy Mac's guitar.

In those days Jimmy played guitar with Quayle's City Ramblers Skiffle Group, top of the bill at theatres from Brighton to Inverness.

Then he played 21 years as a duo with Robin Hall. They made 21 albums, toured the world and filled all the big halls and small folk clubs in Britain.

In more recent years his *Macgregor's Gathering* radio programme on Radio Scotland features the best of Scottish traditional and traditional-influenced music, as well as promoting and supporting creative writing, and the knowledge and maintenance of many aspects of Scottish life and heritage.

PACK YOUR TOOLS AND GO

Written for the Upper Clyde Shipbuilders work-in of 1971.

Before his Robin and Jimmie days he played guitar for Ewan MacColl, backing him on records and singing harmonies. For Ewan's 70th birthday there was a big concert in London, at which the singers included Gordeanna MacCulloch and Dick Gaughan. When Jimmie sang this song, and reached the line about Jimmy Reid, the audience hissed. Jimmie pointed out that, while understanding the response, Jimmy Reid's involvement in UCS was a historical fact. Then he wrote alternative lines for the song. I've given the original here.

PACK YOUR TOOLS AND GO

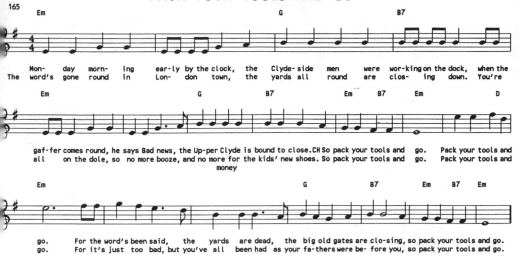

Mon- day morn- ing ear-ly by the clock, the Clyde-side men were wor-king on the dock, when the
The word's gone round in Lon- don town, the yards all round are clos- ing down. You're

gaf-fer comes round, he says Bad news, the Up-per Clyde is bound to close. CH So pack your tools and go. Pack your tools and
all on the dole, so no more booze, and no more for the kids' new shoes. So pack your tools and go. Pack your tools and
money

go. For the word's been said, the yards are dead, the big old gates are clo-sing, so pack your tools and go.
go. For it's just too bad, but you've all been had as your fa-thers were be- fore you, so pack your tools and go.

Then along came a man whose name was Reid.
Says he, we'll win if we keep the heid.
For we've got the brains and the old know-how.
We won't bow down and we won't kow-tow.

Pick up your tools let's go. Pick up your tools let's go.
For we'll make our way without their say,
And keep the hammers ringing.
Pick up your tools let's go.

Here's a word for the men down south.
You're big in the belly and big in the mouth.
You live far away and you don't give a damn
For the life and pride of a working man.

So pack your tools and go. Pack your tools and go.
For we're here to say you've had your day,
It's time that you were leaving.
So pack your tools and go.

You're on the run, your day is done,
So pack your tools and go.

Words by Jimmie Macgregor
Music 'Drill, Ye Tarriers, Drill'

NIGEL DENVER

I was at school with Nigel, the strong lungs in the Allan Glen's Skiffle Group, which did very well in the Carroll Levis talent show at the King's Theatre—the usherettes were astonished at the rows of school blazers filing into the upper circle to support their side—Glen's as an all boys school believed in solidarity, although the winsome girl singer who came second that night tested school loyalty strongly.

Nigel moved south, to Manchester then Birmingham. Like a couple of other singers in this book, Nigel's energy and enthusiasm as a live performer somehow did not translate so well to disc, but I hear he's still singing and getting in trouble.

MAGGIE'S WADDIN

Nigel recorded this on a whole album of Scottish Republican songs produced and mostly written by Jim McLean. The titles tell the story—'Forget The Auld Orange And The Green', 'The English Royal Family', 'The Scottish MP', 'A Parcel of Rogues', 'NAB For Royalty', 'The Wallace' and others. The sleeve notes are by Hugh McDiarmid, who points out that 'Rule Britannia' is a Scots song, and 'God Save The King' is a parody on another Scots song. (No, I don't know which song he had in mind.)

I'd forgotten that 'The Scottish MP' was Jim's song till researching for this book. It is of course very unfair and inaccurate. (MPs get titles, not medals.)

> Oh, I am a Scottish MP from a city grey and black.
> And I'll shut my mouth when I'm in the south
> Just in case they send me back.
> Oh, I'm off to London in the morn, in the morn,
> In Westminster I will be.
> And I'll leave behind my brains and mind and try for an M.B.E.

Jim's 'Maggie's Waddin' got me in various kinds of bother. I was barracked in Mombasa for singing it—not because of its criticism of the Royals at a time long years before it became fashionable—no, because it was a little unkind to the Queen Mother, a great lady and after all a Scot. I was moaned at for singing it in London Folk clubs—'Oh God, another bloody Scot'.

I've printed the song as sung by Nigel, and as printed in *The Rebel Ceilidh Song Book*. As usual some other singers sing differing lyrics, and someone will write and tell me that I've printed the wrong words.

MAGGIE'S WADDIN

Sing a song o' tax and woe, emp-ty poo-ches in a row, Chan-cell-or's col-lect- in dough aa for Ma-ggie's wa-ddin.

Silk and sa-tin, gold la-me, To-ny weirs a lum hat tae, ma suit's in the pawn sae whit-'ll ah dae at the Ro-yal Wad-din?

Maggie flounces doon the aisle, Mither staunds wi forcit smile.
Needs a dose o castor ile, At her dochter's waddin.

Tony's doon on bendit knee, gied up his photographie.
Nae mair burdies will he see efter Maggie's Waddin.

Foreign guests fae near an faur, packed inside Westminster Haa,
Parasites fae France an aa at the Royal Waddin.

Whaur d'ye think they'll honeymoon? Rome, Paree or on the moon?
Withoot a doot it's no Dunoon! Efter sic a waddin.

Noo they're mairrit aff they blow, tae spen a thoosan poon or so.
That's the wey oor money goes for Mrs Jones's waddin.

Back again an help ma bob! Tony hasnae got a job,
Wha will buy the christenin robe? You an me ah'll bet ye.

Royal mince is awfy dear, Tony needs a rise next year.
Up'll go the tax on fags an beer, efter Tony's waddin.

Maggie's taen up fancy cookin, Bird's Nest Soup fae a Chinese book.
An Susie Wong won't hae a look in. Velly nicey wedding.

Sing a song of tax an woe, empty pooches in a row.
Chancellor's collectin dough aa for Maggie's Waddin.

Words by Jim McLean
Music 'Mhairi's Wedding'
Published by Duart Music

ANDY HUNTER

We were at school together, and were both enthralled by the music and songs Morris Blythman introduced us to.

Andy began songwriting early—I've already quoted from his 'Baron James McPhate'. He has written songs about a visit to the dentist, rugby matches, a fight at Aboyne Games and the joys of angling.

He also takes and fills out fragments of old song to give them new life and vigour. His best work in this line is 'King Fareweel', which he learned as a three verse slice of a 'big Jacobite ballad' sung by the great Jeannie Robertson, and turned into nine strong and poetic verses which tell the story of the '45 campaign.

Andy stayed with and studied with Jeannie Robertson, and developed an impressive understanding of the big ballads.

He has become a noted player of the bellows-blown Scots Border Pipes - the 'cauld wind' pipes. Which must make the Highland war pipes the hot air pipes.

KILBOWIE HILL

Andy was sitting one day, his pipes strapped on, leafing through a collection of pipe music called *David Glen's Irish Collection*.

His attention was taken by a beautiful air called 'The Dawning Of The Day'. He married it to words about walking down Kilbowie Hill from where he lived up on Cochno Road above Hardgate.

Luke Kelly of the Dubliners happened to set the same tune to a poem by Patrick Cavanagh to make a song called 'Raglan Road'. Cavanagh also uses 'at the dawning of the day' as a last line to his verses—perhaps he had the tune in mind when he wrote.

Andy Hunter had not heard Luke Kelly's song when he made his own. 'When I did hear it, it shook me rigid. Perhaps the tune makes you think of writing in certain ways?'

'The song takes as its setting a view familiar to all 'Bankies' - the shipyard cranes of John Brown's seen from the top of Kilbowie Hill, which rises above the heart of the town. The Kilpatrick Hills and Cochnae Braes are rural areas well beloved by shipyard and other industrial workers of the area as offering respite from industrial grind and grime.'

KILBOWIE HILL

I was stroll-in doun Kil-bow-ie Hill on a cauld No-vem-ber's day. The morn-in mist hung o- wre me, and the toun was dark and grey. My thochts were wi my bro- ken love, the wound was there to stay. And the ship-yaird cranes they staun their lane at the dawn- in of the day.

I saw her run before me
As she laughed her cares away,
As saft as ony simmer's breeze
Across the Cochnae Braes.
I never knew the love was mine
I chose tae throw away.
And the shipyaird cranes they staun their lane
At the dawnin of the day.

The Kilpatrick Hills my hairt wid fill
Wi tears o' November rain.
Tho' summer sings her ain song, love,
It's never twice the same.
She taught me verse and chorus
But the bonny air's away,
And the win' soughs owre Kilbowie Hill
At the dawnin of the day.

The Queen that lies against the dock
Will shortly sail away.
The sun that shines upon her hull
Will shine through Clyde's clear spray.
I saw the light shine through her eyes
As I wiped her tears away,
And I saw her lyin' beside me
At the dawnin of the day.

Words by Andy Hunter
Music 'The Dawning Of The Day'

DUNCAN MACRAE

J D G Macrae, a lean and lantern jaw followed by a face and voice of wondrous sardonic humour. Born in Glasgow in 1905 of a family who had been crofters in Sutherland. Like many of the songwriters in this book, he was for a time a teacher before the stage caught him.

To my regret I never met him, in Balgrayhill or elsewhere. He had a connection with the Blythmans—a song he wrote called 'My Ain Close'—a parody of 'My Ain Folk', with such glorious lyrics as

> It's oh but ah'm longing for ma ain close.
> It wis nane o yuir wally, juist a plain close.
> An ah'm nearly roon the bend for ma ain wee single-end,
> Farewel tae dear old Gorbals an ma ain close.
> They'll never be forgotten, the days that we lived through.
> When we hung aboot the Gorbals an we sterved on the Buroo.
> Wi the lassies playin peever an the laddies sclimmin dykes,
> An the weemin gaun thir dusters an the polis gaun thir bikes.

Morris Blythman published this song in *The Rebel Ceilidh Song Book '67*, and commented on it that it showed 'a communal conservatism worthy of the best of our traditions opposing a modern sterile bureaucracy.'

WEE COCK SPARRA

Not Duncan's own. Albert D Mackie writes in *The Scotch Comedians* that an Edinburgh lawyer called Hugh Frater sang a much more perjink version in student revues. Frater had learned it 'from an old man somewhere about Stirling'.

Duncan's version, complete with screeching top note, exemplifies a pub singer style particular to the West. Only Billy Connolly on 'Saltcoats Goodbye' takes the singing style further out.

WEE COCK SPARRA

A wee cock spa- rra sat in a tree. A wee cock spa- rra sat in a tree,

A wee cock spa- rra sat in a tree chir-pin a - wa as blythe as can be.

Along cam a boy wi a bow an an arra.
Along cam a boy wi a bow an an arra.
Along cam a boy wi a bow an an arra.
And he shouted 'Ah'll get ye, ye wee cock sparra.'

Ra boy wi ra arra let fly at the sparra,
Ra boy wi ra arra let fly at the sparra,
Ra boy wi ra arra let fly at the sparra,
But he hit a wee man who wiz wheelin a barra.

The man wi the barra cam ower wi the arra,
The man wi the barra cam ower wi the arra,
The man wi the barra cam ower wi the arra,
He says 'Dae ye tak me fur a wee cock sparra?'

The man hit the boy, though he wisny his farra.
The man hit the boy, though he wisny his farra.
The man hit the boy, though he wisny his farra.
An the boy stood an glowered, he wiz hurt tae the marra.

An all this time the wee cock sparra
An all this time the wee cock sparra
An all this time the wee cock sparra
Wiz chirpin awa on the haft o the barra.

'As ah came by the sweetie works'

The canyon streets of Glasgow

Susan McCamley—THIS TOWN
Jim McLean—FAREWELL TO GLASGOW
Alan Cairney—DAEN UP THE FLAT
Gordeanna McCulloch—WEE GALLUS BLOKE
Bobby Eaglesham—SOOR MULK CAIRT
Joe Plunkett—HOT ASPHALT
New Street Song Competition—CULTURE SKIP,
GLESCA, MA YUPPIE MAW

'AS AH CAME BY THE SWEETIE WORKS'

We win some and lose some every time Glasgow turns a new corner.

> The city is changin' a' year and a' day.
> And it's changin' as fast in the night-time.
> For the next buildin's gone, as you lay there and yawned.
> But we a' know that now is the right time.

When I was a teenager the streets of the city seemed like deep canyons. As you walked along you could hardly see the sky, let alone the skyline.

> CHORUS
> So in wi' the crane, and the swingin steel ball
> And oot o' the rubble the factor'll crawl.
> Ta-ta, tae the caves in the canyons.

When the Corpie began dinging doon the tenements, they let the daylight in. As the demolitions spread you began to be able to see the hills that surround the city. When the high rise buildings rose they had great areas of green around them. You felt you could breathe more easily.

> The buildin's were sandstone, the red and the grey.
> But they turned black, wi' a' the fires smokin'.
> Noo the sky's gettin' brighter, the concrete stays white,
> And you don't hear the sparras a' chokin'.

We didn't at first learn about the new problems that had been made. The Fisher family moved out to a wonderful new scheme, all fresh and bright looking. It was called Easterhouse. They held a big bright party to celebrate their new abode.

> Did you love stairheid lavvies: six families tae wan?
> Were the steamie- washed claes never dirty?
> Could you squeeze in a friend, in your wee single-end?
> Was your mother decrepit at thirty?

They moved back to Napiershall Street six months later.

When a couple of years ago I heard Ian Davison's 'Caves In The Canyons' I was startled that he had chosen the same image that I had for the tenement streets. He says he got it from an Edwin Muir poem, and points out that the skyscraper streets of New York were referred to as canyons. I think that must be where I got the idea—a song about New York. Then the skyscrapers came to Glasgow.

So clear oot the middens. Let light in the close.
The high-flats'll beat the diseases.
It's miles tae the ground, but there's grass a' around.
And the watter supply never freezes.
(Written by Ian Davison,To the tune of 'The Thirty Foot Trailer'.)

Ian's song captures well the optimism of those days, and was written as a response to Adam McNaughtan's 'The Glasgow That I Used To Know'. So was Jim McLean's 'Farewell To Glasgow'. Nostalgia will always get you in trouble with people who remember the bad news as well as the good news.

But nostalgia has its own truth, surely? Nostalgia for the recalled feelings of shared identity and mutual help and trust in hardship—doors never locked—except for the door of the most powerful and pungent symbol of all, the cludgie on the stair.

Mind you, the over-sweetness of the old tearjerker 'Ma Ain Wee Hoose' produced more than one parody in its own day.

One famous one, sung widely during the Folk Revival, is 'Ludgin Wi Big Aggie'.

Ah wis ludgin wi Big Aggie, there wis me and ither ten.
We aa slept thegither in a wee bit single end.
There were nae beds ataa, we jist leant against the wa.
And we were all that seek we didnt waken fur a week
In wir ain wee hoose, in wir ain wee hoose.
Last Saturday for dinner we had sossige on a plate.
Ah wis just aboot tae eat it, when the sossige it cried 'Wait!
Afore ye start on me, ah wis born in 1903.'
And ah went stane blin, when the sossige it did rin
Roond wir ain wee hoose, roond wir ain wee hoose.
We had rabbit for wir supper, ah could hardly stand the pain.
In fact, one fellow's snuffed it, and anither's gone insane.
Aggie says it wis ra flu, but I don't think that is true.
For wir tom cat, Prince, has been missing ever since
Frae wir ain wee hoose, frae wir ain wee hoose.

Another version was collected in Greenock just last year.

It wis just a humble placey, but ah'd always paid ma rent
Till the factor had the facey, tae raise it ten percent.
It's a right disgrace, tae pay fur sic a place.
A wee top flat, where ye couldny swing a cat
Wis ma ain wee hoose, wis ma ain wee hoose.
The sanitary's condemned it, he says he'll pull it doon as well.
Ah telt him no tae bother, it wad tumble doon itsel.
The walls are needin paintin, and the windae's needin glass.
An ah canny get hot water cause the biler, it's aa bashed.
But it's ma ain wee house, it's ma ain wee hoose.
(Collected from May Clark by Theatre Seanachaidh.)

In my days at school everyone was required to 'speak correctly'. I envy so much today's young people who are offered the poetry of Tom Leonard and some of the songs in this book. Our mothers, who tried to make us speak properly, had little time for this.

Ma maw's a millionaire.
Blue eyes and curly hair.
See her walkin doon the street wi her big banana feet.
Ma maw's a millionaire.
Ma maw's a millionaire. (Lives in Glebe Street!)
Blue eyes and curly hair.
Sittin among the eskimos playing the game of dominoes.
Ma maw's a millionaire.
(See Page 101 for a modern version.)

Of course our grannie could be expected to stick up for us. A powerful figure, the Glasgow grannie.

A B C, ma grannie caught a flea.
She salted it and peppered it and had it for her tea.

D E F, ma grannie went deaf.
Goin tae the football and shoutin at the ref.

J K L, ma grannie made a smell.
What did she smell like? Not very well.

P Q R, ma grannie bought a car.
She took me oot fur hurlies on the handlebar.

S T U, ma grannie caught the flu
Doin the Hokey Cokey wi a kangaroo.

As Cliff Hanley points out in *Dancing In The Streets* we learned three languages, each with its own grammar, pronunciation, vocabulary and syntax. One was the way we spoke in school, one the way we spoke at home, one how we spoke with our peers in the streets.

If in any of these settings we used the wrong lingo, we would be pulled up sharply. We knew from the moral or physical force employed that the languages of home and school had right on their side, and had been taught that how we spoke among ourselves was wrong. Pure and simple wrong.

The first recognition that the way kids spoke in the streets of Glasgow might have any validity was a wonderful drama series on BBC Radio called *The McFlannels*.

The McFlannels was introduced by a tune called 'The Glasgow Highlanders'.

> Willy, Maisie, Sarah, lazy Uncle Matta,
> Spoke like real folk—well, close enough for those days.
> Washin at the jawbox, layin new waxcloth.
> Never died a winter yet, common five-eighths.
> When you think about it, all the names were cloth.
> McTweed, McTwill, McTapestry, McCotton, McVelvet, McPlush.
> If you know about them, you're rather showin yer age.
> That's right—Friday night. McFlannel was the name.
> Who wrote the McFlannels? Ah, now yer askin.
> Yes, I know the answer cause I bought the books in Paddy's Market.
> First Book Of The McFlannels, McFlannels See It Through.
> Were sittin between a broken clock and a box of superglue.
> Oh, my, me. My, me, ma maw!
> It's terrible tae be auld and no tae be wanted at aa.
> Time we brought them back again, McFlannels Return Tae The Clyde.
> What was that? The writer's name? Helen W Pryde!
> (To the tune 'The Glasgow Highlanders'.)

I've spread some of the 'street songs' of Glasgow through this book. I think they are so called because they belong to no one and to everyone. Kids like them, but so do adults who use them to recall the simple joys of being kids—nostalgia again, filtering out the bad memories.

> Dancin wi a moonman, doon at the Barrowlands.
> Dancin wi a moonman tae McGregor and his Band.
> When the lights are turned doon low, and they play the rock and roll
> Oh, it's smashin dancin wi a moo-oo-oonman.
> (To the tune of 'Roamin In The Gloamin'.)

One place they would be heard in a more formal way would be as a small guiser's performance piece on Halloween night, when the streets were full of scurrying little figures wearing sheets or fancy dress.

Another was in the 'back court concerts', which were often got up by some junior impresario to amuse and control the littler ones under her responsibility perhaps because it was Monday and mother had urgent business in the washhouse.

The other bringers of melody were the back court singers. They sang Scots art songs like 'Urquhart's Fairy Glen' or 'The Rowan Tree', religious songs selected to reflect the religious bias of the street, an occasional old ballad, an occasional modern song.

The ringing acoustic qualities of the back courts made indifferent singers sound better than they were, and if they were rotten, all the more reason to throw them down a penny so they would go and sing badly elsewhere.

> There were three old singers came tae oor back court.
> They smelt quite high and they sang quite low.
> 'I'm afraid, I'm afraid', ma mither said.
> 'We're in for a touch of culture oh.'

When we lived in Paisley Road, Kingston—west of the Gorbals and east of Paisley Road Toll—in the early 1970s we occasionally had a back court singer come round. He had a fine voice and a line in stentorian religious songs like 'Pull for the Shore, fellows, Pull for the Shore, reck not the mounting billows, bend to the oar.'

In the 60s when the Fisher family lived in Napiershall Street Archie heard an unusually good back court singer. He looked out and saw Davey Stewart.

As Hamish Imlach points out, 'Alan Lomax of the Library of Congress considered that Davey's version of 'McPherson's Farewell' was the most magnificent piece of virtuoso singing he had ever heard. And Lomax had recorded Leadbelly, Woody Guthrie, the lot. Yet Davey had to busk in the street till his dying day—at times he'd have to pawn his accordion, pawn his whistle—even pawn his teeth.'

When in 1989 Scottie McLean of Garthamlock won a trophy and a prize of £100 from STREETBIZ, the Glasgow festival of street performers, none of the judges knew his name, although he was their unanimous choice, and had been playing and singing in the streets and back courts of Glasgow since 1945. In recent years he's had a regular pitch on Buchanan Street, playing on two penny whistles at the same time.

84

My favourite street character was a newspaper seller who had a pitch near Central Station, where for years he called out only one headline which fitted the news of any day. 'TERRIBUL TRAGEDY!' he bawled. 'TERRIBUL TRAGEDY!'

Someone should write a song about him.

The *Glasgow Evening Times* decided in August 1990 that it was time Glasgow had some new street songs. The Bank of Scotland agreed.

The entries for the competition avalanched in, and I was lassooed as one of the judges. Some people had miscomprehended the point, and sent in old songs, like

> Mary McGinty bought a penny doll.
> She washed it and dried it, then she let it fall.
> Ma sent for the doctor, the doctor wouldny come.
> Send for the ambulance, rum tum tum.

and

> Ma maw says ah huv tae go, wi ma daddy's dinner-o.
> Champit totties, chewin steak, and a wee bit currant cake.
> Ah come tae a river and a couldny get across,
> Ah peyed five bob fur a skabby auld horse.
> Ah jumped upon his back, his bones gave a crack,
> And ah had tae play ma fiddle till the boat came back.

A few of those sent in you have never seen in print, and you won't find them here either—they are just too frank and fundamental.

I can quote you one, I think.

> Oh, Mrs Macafee, won't you come tae bed wi me?
> Ah'll give you a cup o tea tae keep yer belly warum.

The new songs tended to concentrate on the headline approach to Glasgow 1990 City Of Culture—Pavarotti, Glasgow's Glasgow, Frank Sinatra. Culture rhymes with vulture, grannie with tranny.

My favourite grannie entry came from John Brown, a finalist.

> Ma wee granny thinks Mantovanni
> And this Pavarotti culture stuff is fine.
> She disnae mind Hayden, or even Iron Maiden.
> But she'd rather have Sydney Devine.
> Ma wee granny heard on the tranny
> That drinkin' wine was culturally cute.
> She went oot and bought a caseful, and gied hersel a faceful,
> And noo she's as cultured as a newt.
> Ma wee granny, wi' her boyfriend Big Danny,
> Went tae the Burrell fur the day.
> She said 'It's a pity in this year of Culture City.
> Ye'd think they'd fling this auld stuff away.'
> (To the tune of 'I Love A Lassie')

A dissident view of grannie worship came from M. Forsyth.

> See ma granny, she's an awfy wumman.
> She eats the jam and gie's us the scummins.
> We a' run away when we see her comin'
> And play a gemme o' peever doon in the dunny.

There were lots of general praising songs, like one from Jack Watson.

> Ah'm Glesca-born an' proud o' the fact,
> Ma clothes are torn, for ah'm no' well-stacked,
> But ah'm well-fed, an' very well-bred,
> For ah wis born in Glesca.

Jack also submitted one of the many music-hall style ditties.

> Mrs McKay is comin' frae Skye,
> She'll get steak-pie, an ah'll sit and sigh.
> If she leaves crumbs, ah'll jist take whit comes.
> Anything does for the lodger.

Another came from Marie Murray.

> My name is Hugh, I am a doo, I live in Culture City.
> Go to George Square, you'll find me there, and I'll be sitting pretty.
> I get fed by the punters, I look like Billy Bunter.
> I cannae fly, so here sit I, and watch the world go by.

A music hall approach set to the 'Sailing Up The Clyde' tune which made it to the finals came from Moira McIntosh.

> Sailin' doon the Clyde, sailin' doon the Clyde.
> On the Glesca sludgie wi' a nosepeg by yer side.
> There's a lump comes in yer throat, an' a smell ye canna bide,
> When ye're sailin' on the sludgeboat doon the bonnie banks of Clyde.
> They come from far an' near, the Clyde's beauty to behold.
> The jewels of the west coast, as we sail along, unfold.
> Innellan and Dunoon, and dear sweet Rothesay Bay,
> But a' the folk that bide there keep sendin' us away.

Ellen Bruce, another finalist, used 'Ye Canny Shove Yer Grannie' and a nice line in showing the Glasgow accent, for her song called 'Glasgow—City Of Culture'.

> Ah'm a wee wean fae Glesca, so ah'm ur,
> But ah'm still a culture vulture, so ah'm ur,
> Aw the paintins wir jus magic,
> Leonardo's life was tragic,
> Ah'm goany be a mutant turtle, so ah'm ur!
> The dancin at the ballet, it wis rerr,
> They fairly made the stoor jump aff the flerr,
> Pavarotty did his totty,
> But some o' cultyers grotty,
> an' we went tae Disneyworld fur the Ferr!
> You could sing at Renfrew Ferry, so ye could,
> An' dae the dancin even if yer leg wis wood,
> Oh, ah luved the Peoples Palace,
> An the shows at the Green wer gallus,
> At the circus neerly a' the folk wis nude!
> It was a just pure ded brilliant, so it wis,
> Noo ah ken why ma maw made a' the fuss,
> She took me tae Glesca's Glesca,
> Tho' it wisnae very funny,
> It was a' held doon a dunny, so it wis!

Among the memories of pensioners, one entry came in from Lynsey McDonald, aged 5 1/2 years. I can't tell how much of it is hers, how much is old. What do you think?

> Mind thon day, a bonny bonny day, I met my Auntie Nellie.
> She gave me a penny tae buy some sweets, I bought a wee canary.
> The wee canary flew away, ma Auntie Nellie caught it.
> She caught it by the tail and flung it in the pail.
> Cheeky Auntie Nellie.

SUSAN MCCAMLEY

In July 1990 the Scotia Bar sponsored a Scots Political Song competition. Susan sang this song.

She introduced it by saying 'I like sunshine and I like sailing. I don't know very much about big politics, but I like to write songs about small politics. This song is about this town and the people who live in it, particularly the people who live in Springburn. There's not as many of them as there used to be.'

The feeling of the song is so clearly and honestly expressed I assumed Susan was Springburn bread and buttered.

'No. I was born in Paisley, now I live in Lennoxtown. I work fulltime with teenagers. I was working with a kid from Springburn, and got interested in what was happening to the area.'

Susan has been singing and writing for years. 'No special influences—I like lots of women singers. I write about old men round where I live, newspaper articles, romantic things—whatever interests me.'

She has been working recently to build up her singing and writing career, and hopes to put an album of her own songs together soon.

THIS TOWN

Springburn features in various songs in this book—'The Freedom Come-All-Ye', 'Doon In The Wee Room', 'The John MacLean March'— and was famous for heavy industry, particularly the railway engine works.

Springburn has been getting knocked down and rebuilt for 30 years now.

The Blythmans' ceilidh house in Balgrayhill was swept away in favour of a great rolling wave of concrete housing.

One sad week in 1979 I had in the course of my work each morning to drive around Springburn with an old local gentleman suffering from dementia. Each morning he asked 'What place is this, son?' When I said Springburn he said each time 'My, it's awful changed'.

The latest destruction has been the slicing through of wider and fancier roads to get car commuters from the green belt into Glasgow centre faster. I'm a car driver. I have mixed feelings on the matter.

THIS TOWN

When did you last drive through Spring-burn? Where they're pull-ing all the hous-es down. Hope you nev-er have
to re-turn there be-cause they're cut-ting the heart right out of this town. Right out of this town. CHORUS This
used to be a vill-age on the edge of a ci-ty, look at it now, it's not so pret-ty, right left and cen-tre they're
pul-ling it down to ac-com-mo-date the traf-fic in and out of this town. In and out of this town.

Look at the empty railroad tracks,
The dual carriage-way filled with trucks.
These sidings once were full of trains
But they'll never run here again.

Some of the houses once won a prize for being beyond compare.
Well done Mr Architect! But you never had to live here.

Some of the houses are empty now, some of them are boarded up.
The police only come here by the van-full, and only if they're brave enough.

There's nothing for the kids to do.
They're standing in the hallways, they're sniffing glue.

People jay-walk the carriage-way
Like the same old streets were there.
Next door neighbours have become distant friends
And they talk occasionally, uneasily on the telephone.

Words and music by Susan McCamley

89

JIM MCLEAN

Jim was a radio engineer to trade, and also a pianist. He became the writer of many fine songs—see 'Maggie's Waddin'.

His 'Massacre Of Glencoe' turned up on a recent cassette by Belfast-based singer Heather Innes, marked Traditional. I asked the singer, and she said 'Well, I learned it at school so I thought it must be very old.'

As a producer Jim has created many albums, among them one to support the Upper Clyde Shipbuilders work-in, one of Scottish Republican Songs, and one commemorating the heady days of the Scotia Bar.

I've quoted from Jim's songs earlier. Another fine effort, based on the old Glasgow song 'Three craws sat upon a wa', had such lines as

> The U.S.A. are giean subs away but we dinnae want Polaris.
> Tell the Yanks tae drap them doon the stanks.
> The Cooncil o Dunoon, they want their hauf-a-croon.
> The Clyde says Naw, ye'll hae tae shoot the craw.

Jim did a lot of songwriting with Dominic Behan, another Irish writer who made a home in the West of Scotland, for reviews that Dominic was doing.

Now Jim has 'A lot of writing things I plan to do—books and plays buzzing around in my head. First I have to finish my degree course at poly.'

Because Jim is another who has recently gone back to college—while still running Nevis Records he is undertaking an Honours Degree in Electronics, working on hush-hush ideas in the design of computer peripherals.

FAREWELL TO GLASGOW

Written in response to Adam McNaughtan's 'The Glasgow That I Used To Know'.

'I was brought up in the slums. There's nothing nostalgic for me about remembering seven of us living in a room and kitchen. Adam's song made me feel very upset.'

Adam acknowledges that Jim's song also has a piece of the truth about tenement living, and has been known to sing it 'back-to-back' with his own.

A review strongly praising this song was somewhat marred by a misprint which commented on the line 'Remember the rates and the mice ye once chased'. Very Kelvinside.

FAREWELL TO GLASGOW

Oh where is the Glas-gow I used to know? The te-ne-ment buil-dings that let in the snow. Through the cracks in the plas-ter the cold wind did blow. and the wa-ter we washed in was fif-ty be-low.

We read by the gaslight, we had nae T.V.,
Hot porridge for breakfast, cold porridge for tea,
Some weans had rickets and some had T.B.,
Aye, that's what the Glasgow of old means to me.

Noo the neighbours complained if we played wi' a ba',
Or hunch-cuddy-hunch against somebody's wa',
If we played kick-the-can we'd tae watch for the law,
And the polis made sure we did sweet bugger a'.

And we huddled together to keep warm in bed,
We had nae sheets or blankets, just auld coats instead,
And a big balaclava to cover your head,
And 'God, but it's cold' was the only prayer said.

Noo there's some say that tenement living was swell.
That's the wally-close toffs who had doors wi' a bell,
Two rooms and a kitchen and a bathroom as well.
While the rest of us lived in a single-end hell.

So wipe aff that smile when you talk o' the days.
Ye lived in the Gorbals or Cowcaddens ways.
Remember the rats and the mice ye once chased.
For tenement living was a bloody disgrace.

Words and music by Jim McLean
Published by J B Music

ALAN CAIRNEY

I first met demon songwriter Alan in early 1990 at an open day for the Performing Right Society—the gang that collects songwriters' money for them—in Edinburgh. Alex told me about a song of his that might interest me. I answered by singing 'Tam The Bam' in his ear.

Then Alan went home and wrote a song about the Open Day, and put me in it—

> Then ah met a freen frae Gartmore, young McCrone M.C.P.S.
> An' a fellah ca'd McVicar sang me 'Bampot' wi' finesse!
> Juist at that ah hud ma photy took while Ewan sang awa'
> An ah talked tae Jim McNeilage about problems wi' oor ha'.

I expressed admiration at this dexterity, and he sent me some more songs about curling and cart horses and Scottish gaucho politicians and drunken golf matches.

Then he phoned me about some matter, and left on my answering machine a song which complained about answering machines.

Impressed yet further, I played the tape on a Glasgow KLT local radio show I was doing at the time. Then I got Alan on to the RADIO KLT programme to talk about his songs, the time he almost became the bass player with the Kenny Ball Jazz Band, and sundry other items.

What was the next phone call? That's right, him singing me a song he'd written about his appearance on radio.

DAEN UP THE FLAT

Although I knew by now various songs of Alan's— 'The Baron Of Buchlyvie', 'The Silver Broom', 'Don Roberto', many others about Gartmore and Kippen and other communities—none seemed right for this book.

I phoned him, confident that if he had no Glasgow songs he'd soon write a few. Within a couple of hours he'd called back to sing me one culled from the files.

'Daen Up The Flat' comes from that crackling music hall tradition in which performers could order comic songs made-to-measure. It's no surprise to hear Alan has written the songs for several local pantomimes. He prefers wordplay and comic invention to the heavy characterisation of 'When Father Papered The Parlour'.

DAEN UP THE FLAT

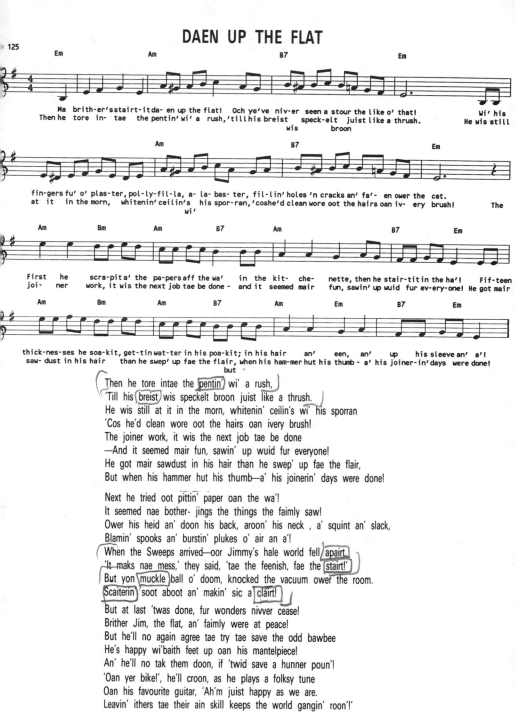

Then he tore intae the pentin' wi' a rush,
'Till his breist wis speckelt broon juist like a thrush.
He wis still at it in the morn, whitenin' ceilin's wi' his sporran
'Cos he'd clean wore oot the hairs oan ivery brush!
The joiner work, it wis the next job tae be done
—And it seemed mair fun, sawin' up wuid fur everyone!
He got mair sawdust in his hair than he swep' up fae the flair,
But when his hammer hut his thumb—a' his joinerin' days were done!

Next he tried oot pittin' paper oan the wa'!
It seemed nae bother- jings the things the faimly saw!
Ower his heid an' doon his back, aroon' his neck , a' squint an' slack,
Blamin' spooks an' burstin' plukes o' air an a'!
When the Sweeps arrived—oor Jimmy's hale world fell apairt,
'It maks nae mess,' they said, 'tae the feenish, fae the stairt!'
But yon muckle ball o' doom, knocked the vacuum ower the room.
Scaiterin' soot aboot an' makin' sic a clairt!

But at last 'twas done, fur wonders nivver cease!
Brither Jim, the flat, an' faimly were at peace!
But he'll no again agree tae try tae save the odd bawbee
He's happy wi'baith feet up oan his mantelpiece!
An' he'll no tak them doon, if 'twid save a hunner poun'!
'Oan yer bike!', he'll croon, as he plays a folksy tune
Oan his favourite guitar, 'Ah'm juist happy as we are.
Leavin' ithers tae their ain skill keeps the world gangin' roon'l'

Words and music by Alan Cairney

GORDEANNA MCCULLOCH

A powerful and entrancing singer, Gordeanna was one of those who caught the song bug from Norman Buchan at Rutherglen Academy. She can hold a late night festival audience in the spell of a Scots big ballad, thrill with a Black American freedom song, or enchant you with a cheeky wee Glasgow number.

Gordeanna sang with the Clutha group for many years, and has made many albums. She has also worked with Ewan MacColl.

Gordeanna is the key figure in the epic EURYDICE women's choir—they have enough vocal power to raise the Mayday marquee off its moorings. They started as the Glasgow Socialist Women's Choir. The name came about because they felt 'Well, we're no the Orpheus Choir'. (For those who have forgotten their Greek gods, Eurydice was the wife of Orpheus.)

WEE GALLUS BLOKE

This song was as I recall sung by a man called Josh Shaw at a party in the house below the Buchans'. The second verse was written by Norman, and the new verses by me.

Gordeanna often ties this song together with a series of 'bottling songs'. You'll still hear 'bottling songs' in the streets of Glasgow— usually on a Friday early evening after the office or factory has stopped work.

You encounter a group of chanting women banging on cooking pans as they lead one of their number wearing a paper cocked hat, draped in coloured crepe paper and bearing a plastic 'chanty'. Every man they meet will be stopped, challenged with 'A penny for a kiss', and expected to contribute substantially more than a penny to the chanty in exchange for a peck on the cheek of the bride-to-be.

Gordeanna sings three 'bottling songs' on Geordie McIntyre's excellent 1972 album on the Topic label called *The Streets Of Glasgow*. One of them was collected from Big Mick Broderick's sister, Jean -

> Ah, ye'll go. Ah, ye'll go. Whether ye want tae or no.
> Wee dirty nappies and wee greetin weans,
> Sign in the book and yer life's no the same.
> Ah, ye'll go. Ah, ye'll go. Ah, ye'll go. Whether ye want tae or no.
> Ye'll go and ye'll get it, ye'll never regret it.
> Ye'll go. Ah, ye'll go. Ah, ye'll go.
> (To the tune of 'Bless Em All'.)

WEE GALLUS BLOKE

As ah came by the swee-tie works, ma hert be-gan tae beat, see- in aa the fac-tory lass-ies com- in doon the street

Wi their flash-y-dash-y pet- ti- coats, their flash- y-dash-y shawls, five and a tan-ner gut- ty boots,"Oh,

we're big gal-lus molls."CH Oh, ye're ma wee gal-lus bloke nae mair. Ye're ma wee gal-lus bloke nae mair.

Wi yer bell- blue strides and yer bun-net tae the side, ye're ma wee gal-lus bloke nae mair.

As ah came by the dancin, ah began tae think.
'Will aa the lassies stand and talk aboot oor Jeanie's mink?
Or will they hae a natter wi me aboot ma past?'
But just when ah got close tae them, they walked away right fast.

NEW VERSES (by Ewan McVicar)

As ah came by the bettin shop ma hert it gied a bang.
There wis Jaickie MacIntyre standin wi his gang.
He tried tae brass-neck it. He said 'Hi, doll, how's it gaun?'
If he thinks he's gettin roon me, the wee rat isny on.

He's ma wee gallus bloke nae mair.
Naw, he's ma wee gallus bloke nae mair.
Wi his hair cut straight, he thinks he's somethin great
But he's ma wee gallus bloke nae mair.

Ma mammie thinks he's magic, ma daddy likes him too.
They didny see him last night in the picture queue.
He says that she's his cousin, but ah'm no ding-a-ling.
And Jaickie's gettin nae mair fun unless he buys the ring.

95

BOBBY EAGLESHAM

I first met Bobby when he lived in Coatbridge, but he was born in a village just outside Glasgow called Gartcosh.

Gartcosh has a wonderful claim to fame, a prime statement about the nature of prejudice and tolerance in Glasgow.

The pub called the Big Shop. This has two doors. You make public your allegiance to Celtic or Rangers by which of the two doors you enter the pub.

Once you enter the pub by either door you find just one large bar. There is no differentiation—you go anywhere in the place you like, stand with whoever you wish. The door you enter by is a symbol of who you are outside, not who you are inside the pub. I wish it had three doors, to allow for football agnostics like me.

Bobby has followed the fortunes of the Folk Revival. He played and sang in a group called The Skerries with Iain Mackintosh and others, then the two of them performed as The Other Half.

Bobby with Dick Gaughan formed a fine folk/rock ensemble gang called Five Hand Reel which made some recordings combining traditional songs with electric excitement. Eventually he went solo, settled down in Cumbria and began running a shop.

Having always painted for pleasure, Bobby is now immersed in a Fine Arts course at Art College.

SOOR MULK CAIRT

Bobby Eaglesham remembers hearing this song sung in his family when he was a toddler. It was not until he heard The Clutha perform it that he realised he should sing it.

When Bobby sings this song, he always comments in a rather deprived way that this is the only song he knows which has his name in it. He's lucky, the only songs with McVicar in them are the one by demon songwriter Alan Cairney I quoted earlier, and a Maggie M'Vicar of uncertain virtue who turns up in the old song 'Glasgow Fair'.

The sour milk cart was drawn at a reasonable pace by one horse, of a steady disposition and 'a certain age'. Giving the driver the chance of clicking with a lass.

The sweet milk cart came at a spanking speed, pulled by two fiery young horses. The sweet milk needed to be in town early, to get into the morning teacups of the well off. The sour milk was used for baking.

THE SOOR MULK CAIRT

CHORUS

Oh, I am a coun-try chap-pie, an ah'm ser-ving at Pol-noon, a wee bit fairm near Ea-gles-ham, that
Wi her cheeks red as ro-ses an her e'en sae bon-ny blue. Glan- cin, en - tran - cin, they
fine auld- fash-ioned toon. Whaur in the morn-in ear- ly, a lit- tle af- ter three
pierced me through and through. She fair-ly won ma fan-cy an she stole a - wa ma hert,
we tak the road richt mer- ri- ly, ma auld black horse and me.
dri-vin in - tae Gles- ga in ma soor mulk cairt.

The other mornin early, as the Borwee I did pass
I happened tae foregaither wi a nice wee country lass.
Says I 'Ma bonny lassie, if ye're gangin ower that airt
Ah'll drive ye intae Glesga in ma soor mulk cairt.'

I raised her up beside me an we soon got on the crack
An wi a smile she told me that her name was Maggy Watt.
I telt the auld auld story while the woods around us rang
Wi the whistlin o the mavis and the blackbird's cheery sang.

I've heard o lords an ladies making love in shady bowers.
An how they woo'd an won amang the roses an the flowers.
But I'll ne'er forget the mornin wee Cupid threw his dart
And made me pop the question in the soor mulk cairt.

Since the lassie has consented gin next term-time comes roon
I mean tae buy a harness plaid an a bonny silken goon.
We're settlin tae get mairret just aboot next August fair
When aa oor auld acquaintances we hope tae see them there.

She'd never had a hurl in a carriage aa her days
An so I did propose tae hae a coach and pair o greys,
But 'Na, na,' quo she, 'The siller's scarce, ye ken we canna spare't
An I'd raither hae a hurl in yer soor mulk cairt.'

Words by Thomas Johnstone
Music 'Jamie Raeburn'

D

JOE PLUNKETT

One of the Irish immigrants to Greater Glasgow, bearing songs and a love of music, Joe now lives in Bonhill. He and his wife Pat are staunch friends of the Faslane Peace Camp.

We met when busking for peace, and formed a peace buskers supergroup to make a cassette of songs as the SCND Buskers, with fellow members and songwriters Ian Davison and Nancy Dangerfield, plus musicians Carol Sweeney and Harry Bickerstaff.

Joe has an unregenerate Irish pronunciation of Glesga patter chorus words. Pat is a sharply witty songwriter—like many Scots she prefers American tunes and references, and doesn't sing any Glasgow songs.

Joe also has a fine edge when he sings Irish uptempo songs.

HOT ASPHALT

The Irish 'navvies' came to Scotland in the 19th century to help dig the new canals, so were called navigators or navvies.

Some of them then got jobs in town, as in this song. The poor relationship between them and the police is recorded in various songs.

The Kelvingrove Museum and Art Galleries, where the navvy got hung, was opened for the 1901 International Exhibition. There is a standing tale that it was built 'back to front'—the debate hinges on whether the impressive entry should have faced The University or the Kelvin Hall.

Ewan MacColl wrote a new song to the 'Hot Asphalt' title and tune, in praise of the Irish black-top layers, and inspired by the Irish road-builders who worked to make the M1 motorway.

He put to the second half of the tune a chorus which goes

> We've laid it in the hollows and we've laid it in the flat.
> If it doesn't last forever then I swear I'll eat me hat.
> I've travelled up and down the world and sure I never felt
> Any surface that was equal to the hot asphalt.

As is the way of singers, Joe Plunkett has added this chorus to the old 'Hot Asphalt' song— he thinks he may have picked it up from singer Tony Nugent or Ted Furey—Finbar's father. Asphalt is by the way pronounced ash-felt in this song.

98

HOT ASPHALT

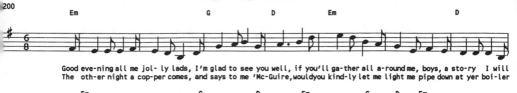

Good eve-ning all me jol- ly lads, I'm glad to see you well, if you'll ga-ther all a-round me, boys, a sto-ry I will
The oth-er night a cop-per comes, and says to me 'Mc-Guire, would you kind-ly let me light me pipe down at yer boi-ler

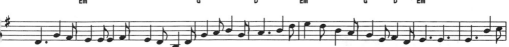

tell. For I'm ov-er here in Glas-gow, and be-gor-ra and be gob, I can whis-per I've a week-ly wage of nine-teen bob. It's a
fire?' He planks right straight with hob-nails naet. 'Here', I, 'Me da-cent man, bet-ter go and bate.' He
him-self in front up so says you'd mind yer

twelve-month come Oct-o-ber since I left my na-tive home, af-ter help-ing in Kil-lar-ney, boys, to cut the har-vest down, but it's
turns and yells 'I'm down on you, I'm up to all your pranks, I know you for a trai-tor in the Tip-per-ar-ay ranks. Boys, I
and

now I wear a guern-sey and a-round my waist a belt, I'm the gaf-fer of the squad that stirs the hot as- phalt.
hit him from shoul-der and I gave him such a welt that he land-ed in the boi-ler full of hot as- phalt.
the

The other night a copper comes, and says to me 'McGuire,
Would you kindly let me light me pipe down at yer boiler fire?'
He planks himself right straight in front, with hobnails up so naet.
'Here' says I 'Me dacent man, you'd better go and mind yer bate.'
He turns and yells 'I'm down on you and up to all yer pranks,
And I know you for a traitor in the Tipperary ranks.'
Boys, I hit him from the shoulder and I gave him such a welt
That he landed in the boiler full of hot asphalt.

We quickly pulled him out again and threw him in the tub
And with soap and warm water we began to rub and scrub.
But, the devil, the thing had tarred him and it turned as hard as stone
And with every other rub you could hear the copper groan.
'I'm thinking' says O'Reilly 'that he's looking like Old Nick
And burn me if I'm not inclined to clean him with me pick.'
'Oh' says I, 'it would be better far to wait until he melts.
And stir him nice and easy in the hot asphalt.'

You can talk about your soldier boys, your sailors and the rest.
Your shoemakers and your tailors, but we please the ladies best.
Sure, the only ones who know the way their flinty hearts to melt
Are the boys around the boiler stirring hot asphalt.
With the rubbing and the scrubbing sure I caught me death of cold
And for scientific purposes me body it was sold.
In the Kelvingrove museum I am hanging in me pelt
As a monument to the Irish stirring hot asphalt.

NEW STREET SONG COMPETITION

Christine MacKenzie's entry in the Evening Times Street Song competition had diagrams showing how the eight skippers should enter and leave the jump area. A night Ward Sister, she and her nurses worked out the moves using lengths of bandages.

To the tune of 'Ten Green Bottles' she wrote

THE CULTURE SKIP

Glasgow's Glasgow—underneath the trains.
People's Palace—go there when it rains.
Transport Museum—Special Olympic Games.
City of Culture with all the famous names.

There was
Rolling Stones and Kylie Minogue, Jason Donovan too.
Torvill and Dean and even the Queen, and Glasgow's Deacon Blue.
There was Pavarotti, and Frank Sinatra came.
Wet Wet Wet and the QE2, they all got in the game.

Nineteen Ninety was City of Culture year.
All the famous people wanted to be here.
They came from Scotland, they came from far and near.
And everyone had lots of fun in City Of Culture Year.

Another finalist, David Scott, didn't know the name of the tune he was using, but I would call it 'Lulu Had A Baby'.

GLESGA

Glesga is the place fur cultyur fur them awe.
If you don't like wee Mozart then go an' tell yur Maw.
She'll tak ye tae the Ballet tae see the Bolshoi dance
Bit she'll hiv tae nick the pay-poke when yer faither's in a trance.

If ye urny workin' Kelvingrove's the place ye want.
Pictures there by Wee Van Gogh an some by Big Rembrant.
Elephants are doon the stair an' lions an' tigers tae.
An' Rennie Mackintosh's stuff is always oan display.

If ha'penny haufs are on your mind, across the road fur you.
Beside the carts an' horses the auld tramcars tae view.
If ye can't 'C'moan Gerraff' it's time ye wurny there.
Or face her wi' the Glesga scowl an' pay yur bloomin' fare.

Glesga's always been a place fur cultyur that is rare.
Seen the pipe-clay in the close and up the bloomin' stair?
Heard the bin men howlin' when you're lyin' in yur kips?
Pavarotti's no a chance—he's had 'is fish an' chips.

MAH YUPPIE MAW

Mah maw's an opera fan.
Pavarotti is her man.
She says that he's a tally man.
That looks a bit like Desperate Dan.
Mah maw's an opera fan.

Mah maw's a bloomin' square.
Frankie S. gets in her hair.
She peyed a hundred fur a seat.
And a' she did was sit and greet.
Mah maw's a bloomin' square.

Maw thinks she's a millionaire
When it comes tae the Glesca Fair.
She took us a' tae Glesca Green.
And left hersel' withoot a bean.
But she felt like a millionaire.

Mah maw spent lots o' dough.
She took us tae the Bolshoi show.
We could hardly see when we got in.
But oh they mad a helava din.
Mah maw spent lots o' dough.

Maw's no' a millionaire,
But says that she disnae care.
1990's left her skint.
The Year Of Culture's cost a mint,
But she'll aye be back fur mair.

Words by Sadie Taylor
Music 'Ma Maw's A Millionaire'

The winner of the Bank Of Scotland and Evening Times 1990 Street Song Competition. Sadie says she was only hoping for the free tickets for the Street Song show. Instead she made a song—the first she has ever written—that gives a speedy sharp-angled tour round 1990 in Glasgow.

'When I get a couple of drinks on a Saturday'

The Scotia Music Hall

Iain Mackintosh—I WISH I WAS IN GLASGOW
Ewan McVicar—TAM THE BAM
Roddy McMillan—GOVAN BILLIARD HALL
SONG
David R Clark—BARROOM MOUNTAINEERS
Brendan McLaughlin—DOON IN THE WEE
ROOM
The Unknown Comedian—THE BROOM BLOOMS
BRAWLY
Alex Campbell—NANCY WHISKY

'WHEN I GET A COUPLE OF DRINKS ON A SATURDAY'

When I returned to live in Glasgow in 1968 I quickly found my way to Ye Olde Scotia Inn at the foot of Stockwell Street.

In the Wee Back Room there I found a company of people dedicated to the pleasure of the song. Instrumentalists hardly existed in those days.

The pub had its own newspaper, run at the time by Freddie Anderson and Jimmy Blackburn. This unprincipled publication once ran a competition to find a better name for a group I then played in—what was so wrong with Ba'heid McBear as a name?

The Scotia commanded the presence of any professional folkie who was visiting town. It had the finest choral singing—a hundred-voiced harmony of 'Pleasant And Delightful' is a delight never heard by the generation which has grown up with the Plague Of Fiddlers.

Best of all, in the Wee Back Room twenty people could sit on top of each other and compete in songs, story telling and general hilarity while late-comers pressed their noses against the glass outside.

Its popularity was its downfall. Mr Plod, seldom a comprehender of innocent mirth, became convinced that the Wee Back Room was a dope-dealer's den. Anyone could have told him that the herbal substances and Oxo cubes were being retailed either in the Gents' or round the corner in front of the Chicken Factory—which by the way was not a pub but a chicken factory, wholesale but not manufacturing.

The law leant heavily upon the owners, and the W B R was shut. The folkies protested. They organised a boycott and put an official picket on the door. The picket was changed every hour by a relief from The Wee Man or the Victoria Bar. The picket lasted for weeks.

The picket was only on the left hand door of the Scotia of course. The right hand door belonged exclusively to the Blue Angels bikers, who patronised the right hand side of the pub and tolerated the odd noises issuing from the left.

The polis won the day. The Wee Back Room never reopened.

Like many others I didn't reenter the Scotia for many years. When I did so in 1987 it was to view and as it turned out compete in a Chorus Singing Competition, part of the Glasgow International Folk Festival. I stood in the open performance space that had once been the Wee Back Room and gave of my best.

I realised afterwards that I had entered and left the pub by the Blue Angels' door.

The Olde Scotia had been through a change or two before my time. Next door to it had been the Scotia Music Hall, a little dun-coloured oldfashioned box of a place which burnt down some 30 years ago, which must have hammered the pub's business severely, and deprived it of fascinating company.

Before that happened I was honoured to be allowed backstage to meet Middle Francie of the famous McPeake family, singers and instrumentalists of renown from Northern Ireland.

They were there performing as part of a touring Irish show. They opened the second half themselves, then played to accompany two champion Irish stepdancers who were so weighed down by the clanking chestful of medals each wore that the step jigs were almost at funeral pace.

Afterwards Middle Francie made an astute observation or two about Scots songs to Ray Fisher and me, then told us that while it was all very well for us to be singing 'them bothy ballads like 'The Barren Rocks Of Delgaty' we should turn our attention to the big and serious songs of Scotland.

We did our best to oblige, but were always tempted by the 'small songs'.

> At Glasgow Cross I met a wee lass.
> Says I 'Ma wee lass, are ye willin tae go?
> Tak share of a gill!' She said 'Sir, I will.
> For ah'm the wee lassie that never said no.'

When considering music hall in Glasgow, it would seem to anyone but a Glaswegian that I have no option but to print 'I Belong To Glasgow' in this book. Except that I have never heard anyone except paid entertainers sing it in Glasgow!

In the Blythman ceilidh house in Balgrayhill one night were some pleasant American visitors. The songs were good, but eventually one of the guests said 'We're rather puzzled that you have not yet sung your own local song for us.'

We had been singing them our own local songs all night—which one had we missed out? 'I Belong To Glasgow!' There was an awkward silence, and an explanation along the lines of 'We don't play that kind of music here, stranger.'

Why don't we sing it? It's a fine song. Perhaps it is too nakedly honest about not feeling good about yourself unless you are drunk.

Maybe we resented the fact that it was written by a Dundonian, Will Fyffe, and the verses and 'patter' more fit the cliche of the tight-fisted Aberdeen man than the openhanded Glasgow drunk.

If your money you spend, you've nothing to lend
Well, that's all the better for you.
When you're teetotal you've got a rotten feeling that everybody's your boss. Why should these bloomin millionaires have all the money? Give it to me!

Assumptions about what it's appropriate to sing can often land you in confusion. Jim Daily and I joined forces one evening with some members of the Laggan group to entertain some visiting Leningrad workers, at the request of the Scottish Soviet Friendship Society.

Things were at the time rather sticky on the superpower front. We diplomatically decided to avoid any American songs. During the interval the workers borrowed our guitars. And launched into the Simon and Garfunkel Songbook.

Will Fyffe wrote another music hall 'Glasgow' song—'Sailing Up The Clyde'. Looking at the original sheet music I am astonished to find that instead of 'Back to Bonnie Scotland where your ain folk bide' the text says 'Back to Bonnie Scotland where your ain folk died'. A miscomprehension by an English copyist, I fear. It gives an extra layer of meaning to 'There's a lump comes in your throat, and a tear you canny hide.'

The major claim to fame of the old Scotia Music Hall was that Harry Lauder, an Edinburgh or to be more precise a Portobello man, had his very first professional engagement there. I believe he was at the time an 'Irish' comedian, this being the fashion of the day.

At the end of his week's engagement the Scotia proprietor, Mrs Bayliss, is said to have handed him his fee and advised him to go home and practise.

Lauder later turned down the offer of 'I Belong To Glasgow' on the grounds that he could not sing a song glorifying drink. When it was pointed out that he sang 'A Wee Deoch An Dorus', he answered that he always emphasised the word wee—he was preaching moderation.

These days folk clubs are always in licensed premises. Is it still against the bylaws to sing in public bars? The rule was music could be licensed in the lounge but not the public. Something to do with religiously bigoted songs again.

Although the Corner House and the Glasgow Folk Centre were dry, we had learned the painful truth about drinking and getting drunk before we were old enough to drink. Going into a pub was however a different matter.

I first entered a pub months after I became 18. There was sawdust on the floor!

Ah'm gettin tired of gettin drunk,
Ma mind's fillin up wi junk.
This drinkin life isnae all it's cracked up tae be.
When I was a lad I used to get a kick from sawdust on the floor.
I'd pretend I was John Wayne or Humphrey Bogart,
I don't think that way any more.
I wish that I'd still got
Half the money that I've poured doon ma throat.
This drinkin life isnae all it's cracked up tae be.

It is surprising how many professional folksingers I know are now non-drinkers. And sad how few of them are still married to the women they started out with.

It is surprising to me how little pub violence I've seen over the years. There was a principle in the speakeasies of Prohibition Chicago that if a fight started the band were exempt from being punched or shot as long as they kept playing. I was reminded of this excellent idea one night in the small Derry Treanor's pub that used to be opposite the Citizens' Theatre in Gorbals Street.

The group Ba'heid MacBear was augmented for the occasion by a guy who played rhythm with a pair of drumsticks on a metal plate set into a wooden base. He had got us the gig!

In the small lounge we were doing quite well, but on the small stage we'd a view of the bar, and of both the doors—the bar was on a corner. The doors were of the bat-wing Wild West saloon type.

It did not occur to me to worry about this to begin with.

We played mostly Irish tunes and songs—that was the engagement. We may even have changed our name to The Mountaineers Of Mourne or some such for the event. Audience members got up to do their party pieces. One young woman sang 'Honky Tonk Angels', with all the extra Hs that singing style requires—'High didaint h-know God made H-Honky H-angels'—to the annoyance of her sister, who had herself intended to sing it. Their father, a small widower in his best black suit, calmed them down.

Then a disagreement began, outside the pub. Every now and then a body would come flying in through one of the bat-wing doors, pick himself up and dash out again into the fray. Soon a body would come flying through the other set of doors. No-one in the lounge took any notice.

The Honky Tonk singer came back agitated from a trip to the Ladies. 'Da! They're killin Shuey oot there!' Da reassured her, and went out to the street to play peacemaker.

Within two minutes he came flying in, his nose bloodied, and scrambled back out to continue the affray. It went on for an hour. There was never any sign of police intervention. We kept playing. Eventually hostilities petered out so that the combatants could get their carryouts bought before the pub closed.

At the end of the night everyone stood up, and the metal plate drummer hissed that we had to play the National Anthem—the Irish National Anthem. We were in fortune's hand. Jim remembered—he thought—that 'The Soldier's Song' was the right one. This seemed much too appropriate to be correct, but we had nothing to lose but a quantity of blood.

He was right. Thanks be. They asked would we play there again the next week, but we thought we had a date arranged elsewhere. We said we'd phone them.

> My wee lad's a sodjer, he lives in Maryhill.
> He goes tae the pub on a Saturday night and buys a half a gill.
> He goes tae the kirk on a Sunday, half an oor too late.
> Pulls the buttons aff his shirt an pits them in the plate.

Or

> Our wee school's a fine wee school, the best wee school in Glesga.
> The only thing that's wrang wi it is the baldy-heidit maister.
> He goes tae the pub on a Saturday night, goes tae the church on Sunday.
> Prays tae the Lord tae give him strength tae murder the weans on Monday.

I love these 'street songs'. They aren't fragments, they're complete songs that happen to last one verse.

> There is a happy land, down in Duke Street Jail.
> Where all the convicts stand tied tae a nail.
> Ham and eggs ye never see, dirty watter fur yer tea,
> There we live in misery—God Save The King!

One of the music hall records I have on very long term loan from Willy Gallacher works off the same idea to make a full length number about 'The big mansion house called Barlinnie Ho-tel'. Another disc is a six minute recitation about 'Auld Glesga On The Clyde', a parody of the heroic cum patriotic numbers that the halls loved, but this time the noble soldiers are not dead, but dead drunk. 'Under the affluence of incohol!'

I was ruminating one day on why 'Nancy Whisky', a song about losing seven years of your life in a haze of booze, should be sung as a merry little ditty. I began to rewrite the words and tune as a sad reflective song with Nancy as the enticing spirit of alcohol, loved and hated simultaneously by the dependent drinker.

Some of my verses are slight variations on the original. Some are new -

> Come landlady, serve an order. Then tell me what there is to pay.
> 'Here's your hat and there's the door. You'll get no more, so on your way.'
> Who's the queen of all dream weavers? Who took my heart? Who took my hand
> And led me down the rocky road then left me here in No Man's Land?
> All you lads of Glasgow city, you know not what your life may be.
> Beware of Whisky, Nancy Whisky, she'll ruin you as she ruined me.
> Still I love her, I'll forgive her, I'll go with her, follow Nancy Whisky.

Let's not sadly follow whisky down the rocky road.

Instead, let's cheerfully join in protest against the excesses of 'The Means Test Man', a bogey man of the Thirties who came back to haunt Glasgow in the Eighties. The song has all the gallusness and bounce of the music hall.

> Ah'm no the factor or the gas man, Napoleon or Ronald Coleman.
> When you hear me rat-tat-tat upon yer door,
> Have ye money in the bank or money in the store?
> Ye better look out or else ah'll get ye.
> Try and dodge me if ye can,
> For ah'm neither Santa Claus nor Douglas Fair-banks,
> I am the Means Test Man.

109

IAIN MACKINTOSH

One of the many good performers around in the late 60s, Iain has grown in authority and professional stature over the years. Now he enriches our listening like fine and mellow wine, and has impressive good taste in songs.

Iain was a pawnbroker who sang and played a long-necked banjo in bands like The Islanders, The Skerries, and The Other Half.

Then he went professional as a solo singer.

'Every night I don't have to worry that the police will phone to say— You're the keyholder, the pawnshop alarm is ringing, you'll have to come down here—that's a night off for me!'

Iain is another who mostly works abroad. 'It's become the bread and butter, and Scotland's become the 'in between the tours' stuff.'

He has made eight solo albums to date, plus two jointly with Hamish Imlach—he and Hamish sometimes tour together.

He and Billy Connolly are both banjo enthusiasts.

I WISH I WAS IN GLASGOW

He's so good on comic songs few people remember that Billy Connolly has a nice line in wistful numbers, like 'Everybody Knows That', and his fine song about a squaddie injured in Northern Ireland, 'Sergeant Where's Mine?'

> You talk of computers, and sunshine and skis.
> Ah'm asking you, sergeant, where's mine?

Billy recorded 'I Wish I was In Glasgow' on an album called *A Change Is As Good As Arrest*.

Iain, with Billy's permission, has rewritten the last verse. You can find his version on an album on the Gallus label called *I Was Born In Glasgow*—the title comes from the first line of Billy's song.

> My grannie brought the family up from the time we lost our mum.
> My father was a good man and he made me all I am.
> There was always bread and butter, there was sometimes even jam.
> And there was so much to learn along the road.

I WISH I WAS IN GLASGOW

I wish I was in Glas-gow with some good old friends of mine. Some good old rough com-pan-ions and some good old smooth red wine. We'd talk a-bout the old days and the old town's sad de-cline and drink to the boys on the road. CH. That great old place I miss so much has seen much bet-ter days And still we talk a-bout it as we go our se-par-ate ways. Oh but Glas-gow gave me more than it ev-er took a-way and pre-pared me for life on the road.

I was born in Glasgow, near the centre of the town,
I would take you there and show you but they've pulled the building down,
And when I think about it it always makes me frown.
They bulldozed it all to make a road.

My granny was a cleaner, my grandad drove a tram.
My father was an engineer, he made me all I am.
They have seen the city come and go, still they give a damn.
There's so much to learn along the road.

Words and music by Billy Connolly
Published by Rocket Music

EWAN MCVICAR

Me masel. The story of my involvement in and learning about the music of Glasgow is spread through this book.

I was one of those that Morris Blythman taught in Glasgow. He said to all of us 'Go and write your good song.'

Like many others I believed in Morris—one of the two great men I have met in my life. I went away and wrote my good song, called it 'Talking Army Blues', and thought 'That's that'. I didn't write another song for seven years.

I gradually developed songwriting, along with poetry and other suspect activities.

I've indulged myself to the point of cramming a few songs of my own into this book. I confess it, and ask for several other crimes of addition and omission to be taken into consideration.

TAM THE BAM

This song came out of a few characters I know or have known in Glasgow pubs. They fasten on and cling for the price of a drink—always bad news, and yet with enough charm and rueful awareness of themselves to stop you refusing to know them at all.

I wrote it at a time when the tune was an almost forgotten Mexican folk song, relegated to TV car commercials. The stories are exaggerated versions of true events.

Any time I sing it, someone comes up, says 'Didn't you write that song about—?'—then realises I don't even know the person. There are many many Tam The Bams in the West of Scotland.

The song reached the final six out of many thousands in a National competition called SONGSEARCH. As Hamish Imlach says about 'Cod Liver Oil', I was amazed that anyone outside Clydeside could understand it.

At the time of the final the obscure Mexican folk song was at the top of the British Top Twenty. I was marked down for lack of musical originality.

I won one hundred pounds in SONGSEARCH, and used the money to start making a record called *I Was Born In Glasgow, Gallus Glasgow Songs*.

So knowing several Tams has brought me some good fortune to add to the grief.

TAM THE BAM

2) You tap hard men for fi- vers, then you for- get to pay them, so you get me to
3) You go out with some young thing, then get in-volved with her ma- mmy.

cool them then you try them out for an-oth - er five, it's a won- der to
The tan - gle you're in is quite ab- surd, you're en - gaged to
fif - teen differ-ent birds, and mar-ried to

me that you sur- vive. You're a CHORUS bam - pot bam- pot what a bam - pot bam - pot.
three more, mark my words, you are a

1) Tam you're a bampot. The original bampot.
You think that you're clever but you're not, you're just a
CHORUS
Bampot bampot What a bampot bampot

4) You go out on a bender. Then you go on a berkie.
You break into some houses, break into some cars.
Break into some pub for a few more jars.
The polis arrive, you wrestle the lot.
Next morning in court you blame it all on the war wound you never got.

5) And while we're on the subject,
When you borrowed my wagon the other night
Did you notice that something's gone wrong with the lights?
I mean, the left side's smashed to bits, the bumper's bent and the door doesn't fit.
Oh aye? You had a wee bit bump? Whose name did you give, you stupid lump?
I've had a summons just arrive to say I'm being done for dangerous driving.

6) I wish I'd never met you.
You come into the pub when you're flat stony broke.
Think I'll buy the booze if you tell the jokes.
I'm telling you Tam it's time you went.
The council's looking for last year's rent.
The tally men are forming a posse. Your mothers-in-law are getting cross.
The Broo's put the special squad on your tail. You're on your tod when it comes to the bail.
Take it from me, your former friend, you're down the tubes and round the bend. You are a

Words by Ewan McVicar
Published by Gallus Music

RODDY MCMILLAN

A gifted and much-loved actor—the classic Para Handy, and a magnificently seedy Glasgow private eye.

A playwright, including *All In Good Faith* and *The Bevellers*. A mean songwriter—look at 'Yuri Gagarin'.

His 'Johnny Ramensky' song begins

> There was a lad in Glasgow town, Ramensky was his name

so it's been suggested it is a Glasgow song and should be in this book. But the rest of Ramensky's story happens in the army and in Peterhead Prison where he broke out a record number of times—I think it's a Peterhead song.

While not having a distinctive singing voice, Roddy had an actor's way with a song—see 'Jamie Foyers'.

For all actors occasional unemployment is part of the job. They even have a special word for it—it's called 'resting'. One of my claims to fame is that I once stood in the same broo queue as Roddy McMillan. In the Sauchiehall Street broo.

THE GOVAN BILLIARD
HALL SONG

I heard this song first sung on a record by Ewan MacColl, at a time when I lived on the edge of Partick on the north side of the Clyde. Govan was just across the river, but as distant and mysterious as Samarkand.

Govan I have in adult life got to know, with its Viking gravestones, the Pearce Institute and a strong rebuilding of shattered streets.

At the time the song was written snooker was a raffish game played in billiard halls, which were dusty dim dens of who-knew-what depravity. To suggest someone had gained their education in billiard halls was to insult them indeed.

Now snooker is a highly respected money earner—I would not be surprised to learn it is an Olympic sport.

But this song still conjures up a scene of smoky wild West shootouts with never a trace of women present.

114

GOVAN BILLIARD HALL SONG

Now Go-van is a bus-y place u-pon a Fri-day night, and the bill-iard halls down there are bus-y too,

and there's ma-ny a strong-ly fan-cied lad been rat-tled in a fight for fidd-lin' with col-ours and the cue.

CHORUS Oh dont stand and look a-round when the cues are up-side down and the balls are fly-ing fast far and near, the

For whe-ther you're tae blame you'd be bet-ter safe at hame, when they're hand-in' out the stit- at yur ear. from -ches

Now 'twas on a certain Friday I went to a saloon
For I'd heard some fancy things about this dive.
So I moved up to a table where two boys were trying hard
To win three sets of snooker out of five.

There were nearly three-score Govan boys with bunnets to the fore
Standing round upon the benches looking grim,
For the wire had got around that one lad was two sets down
And his chances now were geting rather thin.

One half of this mob had bet their dough upon the losing guy
And the rest were on the boy whose game was made,
But the leary losing punters know that when the game was by,
The other mob just weren't getting payed.

Now, the cool-dab lad, the winning boy was lined up for the kill,
He was stickin' home the points in fives and threes,
When the losing rascal calls, as he jungles up the balls
That's all, the gem's a bogie, if you please.'

Words and music by Roddy McMillan

115

DAVID R CLARK

On the same *I Was Born In Glasgow* album that held 'Doon In The Wee Room' I sang enthusiastically a Glasgow hiker's ballad I'd heard in Morris Blythman's house in the 1950s.

When interviewed by the Mr Glasgow columnist of the Evening Times I mentioned that I had been unable to find any trace of the writer's name.

The floodgates opened. The poems and songs of Davey Clark, a shipyard welder to trade, are still highly valued by the old guard of the hiking fraternity. As well as 'Barroom Mountaineers' he had written another song I'd heard in the Blythman house—' Far away in the wilds of Croftamie'.

I received several offers of copies of a handproduced set of David R Clark's poems, entitled *Rough Rhymes Of The Road*. The Robert Service influence is clear, but Davey had a Glasgow lilt—

> Danny, Danny, Danny Devaney
> Jersey and denims patched up by his grannie
> Danny could sit with a pint and ca' canny
> While we drunk a hauf and a beer in a wanny

Soon I learned where David Clark had lived in Rutherglen, and was able to contact his sisters—David had died some months earlier.

BARROOM MOUNTAINEERS

Pleased at my discovery of authorship, I began to play a game with folk enthusiasts of my own vintage, asking them who wrote the song, acknowledging their puzzlement and triumphantly announcing my findings.

Till one night I met with John Dillon, musician and singer, Rutherglen worthy. 'A poser, John. Who wrote the Barroom Mountaineers?'
John looked at me, surprised I should ask. 'Davey Clark, of course. We used to drink in the same pub.' The trick is knowing who to consult.

Many singers admire the sentiments and priorities of this song—the idea of going hillwalking but never getting out of the pub. I have heard the great Matt McGinn rousing an audience to blow the roof off with this number.

The tune uses many phrases from the orchestral signature tune for *Doctor Finlay's Casebook*, but David Clark's song is earlier in date.

BARROOM MOUNTAINEERS

1) In Drymen Square so fair and fine there stands a shop that sells good wine. It's full of whis-key, wine and beer, and so are the Barroom Moun-tain-ee-ee- ee- ee- eers. We're the Barroom Moun-tain-eers.

4) Dont be a-fraid to look us o -ver, we are ve- ry sel-dom so- ber, And when we've had e- nough for four You'll nev-er see us on the floor, But it's up to the bar and yell for mo-o-o-o-ore. We're the Barroom Moun-tain-eers.

2) If you hear a tally-ho, tally-ho, tally-ho,
In the middle of the night, in the middle of the night.
Don't tremble so, dear hostelite.
Just close your eyes and have no fear,
It's only a drunken mountaineer.
We're the Barroom Mountaineers.

3) We've never ever climbed a great big hill
And we hope tae hell we never will.
For the highest we've climbed is a windae sill.
We're the Barroom Mountaineers.

5) From the shores of Balmaha
To the hills of Aberfoyle,
From Drymen Square to Glasachoile.
We're famous everywhere we go,
As a shower of drunken so-and-sos.
We're the Barroom Mountaineers.

Words and music by David R Clark

The tune changes for each verse. For a full idea of the tune, find a singer
or listen to Gallus 102, *I Was Born In Glasgow.*

117

BRENDAN MCLAUGHLIN

Writing notes for a record, I asked 'Who wrote this gem? Quin's Bar in Springburn no longer exists, but I believe the Quin family are still in the business, in faraway Bishopbriggs.'

I heard from Brendan McLaughlin, part proprietor of the Scotia Bar, singer and songwriter. 'The song was written by my grandfather, Daniel McLaughlin. We still have the manuscript of it.'

The connections are surprising. The Wee Room of the song was in Quin's Bar in Springburn, but the Scotia too had a famous Wee Room. Brendan's father, Tony, remembers the names of the men who had identified seats in Quin's Wee Room, now Tony works part-time in the Scotia. He once belonged to a singing group called the Four Kelvins and with them performed in the Old Scotia Music Hall. Tony is also a songwriter.

THE WEE ROOM

There is in the Glasgow folk scene a reluctance to believe that the writer of the Wee Room song has been identified. People seem to prefer the idea of an unknown composer, so they can feel the song in some way belongs to them, to the streets of the city.

But the McLaughlin family have no doubts. They have a copy of the song that includes the extra verses that Ian Davison heard sung once 10 years ago in a rugby club. Daniel McLaughlin was 'bard to Quin's bar', and the family have other pieces written by him, eg 'Burns Night In Quin's'. The family copy of the song has various small differences that suggest it is the original version.

Daniel McLaughlin was born of Irish parents who lived in Springburn Road. He wrote poetry, was active in the Gaelic League, played the fiddle and was a champion singer.

His poetry was religious in tone, and he 'was not proud of The Wee Room or his other songs, which he considered ditties, written to be performed on one special occasion then put aside.'

The tune is not original. I mentioned my interest in it to John Eaglesham of the Mitchell Library.

'Funny', he said. 'I was watching an old Laurel and Hardy film on TV recently. A cowboy appeared and began to sing a song 'Down in the forest, under the trees'. To the same tune!'

In part because of the 'controversy' over the writer, Brendan has not learned the song, nor does his father sing it. 'Doon In The Wee Room' still belongs to the Glasgow folk fraternity at large. But in this book I wanted to link it to Brendan, a third generation Glasgow songwriter.

DOON IN THE WEE ROOM

CHORUS Doon in the wee room underneath the stair, ev-ery-body's hap-py, ev-ery-bo-dy's there and we're aa ma-kin mer-ry, each in his chair, doon in the wee room un-der-neath the stair.

When ye're tired and wea-ry, and ye're feel-in blue, don't way tae sor-row, I'll tell ye what tae do. Take a trip tae Spring-burn, find Quin's Bar there, and go doon tae the wee room un-der-neath the stair.

give

A king went oot ahuntin, his fortune for tae seek,
He missed his train at Partick, went missin for a week.
Oh, after days of searchin, sorrow and despair.
They fun him in the wee room underneath the stair.

If yer team has won the day, and ye want tae cheer
Take a trip tae Springburn and order up a beer.
Have yersel a bevvy, gie yersel a terr.
Doon in the wee room underneath the stair.

When ah'm auld and feeble and ma bones are gettin set
Ah'll no get cross and grumpy like other people get,
Ah'm savin up ma bawbees tae buy a hurly chair
Tae tak me tae the wee room underneath the stair.

Extra verses from the McLaughlin family

What a jolly party, never better found.
Drinks upon the table, friendship all around.
Scottish, English, Irish, Welshmen too come there.
They gather in the wee room under the stair.

Where do all the flies go in the wintertime?
Many people wonder, but I don't care a dime.
I just know where I go to, when I've the cash to spare.
Straight into the wee room under the stair.

King Solomon was a gay lad, he'd forty wives they say.
I've always found that one wife was plenty any day.
So I don't envy Solly, with all his wives so fair.
For he never had the wee room under the stair.

Columbus was a brave man, he sailed the ocean blue.
T'was he that found America, if history books are true.
All honour to Columbus, but more famous I declare
Was the bloke that found the wee room under the stair.

Words by Daniel McLaughlin

119

THE UNKNOWN COMEDIAN

I used to be quite confident I had heard this song on a record by music hall artiste Harry Gordon. Now I'm coming round to the notion that it was Hector Gordon.

After all, Harry Gordon was an Aberdeen comedian, the 'Laird Of Inversnecky' while I have to hand a record of Hector Gordon singing 'Sauchiehall Street'. Much closer to home!

I learned the 'Broom Blooms' song from a 78 rpm record, bought in the Barras by music hall enthusiast Willy Gallacher. Lent to me for a while many years ago.

Willy made a practice of never paying more than sixpence for a record - sixpence was the going rate in the Barras unless the singer was Harry Lauder, in which case it went up to a shilling. Willy never bought any Harry Lauder records, which puzzled Barras stallholders greatly. It wasn't just the cost—he already had all the Harry Lauder records he wanted.

I haven't seen Willy in years, and still have a number of other choice discs belonging to him—including 'Glasgow's Tuppenny Tram'. 'Don't trade your hoard for a Daimler or Ford Like the heroes of Uncle Sam. Now Lachie McKinnon is keepin us winnin wi Glasgow's Tuppenny Tram.'

And there's 'Dear Old George's Square', 'A Sail Doon The Watter' and 'Glesga On The Clyde' Pts 1 and 2. Give me a phone, Willy.

THE BROOM BLOOMS BRAWLY

The Performing Right Society cannot tell me who wrote this song.

The references date it in the 1930s. Bridgeton MP Jimmy Maxton's flowing hair was as famous as his ILP politics. When the song was written Gracie Fields was clearly known in Glasgow as the singer of the screeching 'Biggest Aspidistra In The World'—her sweet-voiced top notes in film parts were to come.

A place hung about with myth and magic was and still is Auchenshuggle. Since childhood I have believed that Auchenshuggle lay somewhere on the bus route between Partick and Clydebank, and that I had passed through it hundreds of times without ever knowing its exact whereabouts. I have just been told Auchenshuggle is away out London Road, south of Tollcross. They say it's always been out there!

But there is no sign anywhere to say you are entering or leaving Auchenshuggle, and I have never ever met anyone who lives or has lived there—Brigadoon or Shangri-la?

THE BROOM BLOOMS BRAWLY

CHORUS I love the lass- ies, ah'm gaun tae wed them aa, when the bloom brooms braw-ly on the bon-nie Broom-ie-law. But in the mean- time we'll hae tae sail a-wa till the broom blooms braw-ly on the bon-nie Broom-ie-law. I have a bon-nie lass-ie, Brig-ton'sher ad-dress, and Jim-my Max-ton's writ-ten us tae wish us baith suc-cess. He's gaun tae get his hair cut just tae gie's a new mat-tress, and I love my lass-ie, oh she's fine.

I have anither lassie, and she lives in Pollokshields.
To nobody in beauty and in charm my lassie yields
She's a face like Tommy Lorne, and a voice like Gracie Fields
But I love my lassie -'In the name!'

I have anither lassie and she lives in Auchenshuggle.
She canna learn tae haud her tongue, it aye goes wiggle-wuggle.
I tried to put ma word in, but ah've given up the struggle,
But ah love ma lassie aw the same.

I have anither lassie and she lives in Kelvinside.
To hear the way she speaks you'd really think the lassie's tried
To make believe that Glasgow's on the Thames, and no the Clyde.
But Ay adore may girlfriend—Faincy thait!

I have anither lassie and she lives in Auchentoshan.
Last Halloween she told me that I was her wee galloshen.
Her face is white and beautiful, but her lugs is needin washin.
But I love my lassie all the same.

ALEX CAMPBELL

I first met Alex in London in 1960. He had just returned from Paris where he had been a busking blind blues singer, complete with white stick.

He had a miraculous recovery in London, and became a folk singer. Alex always mixed his songs, and loved them all. He recorded albums of cowboy songs, albums of Scots ballads, bluegrass and blues and blue material and a blooper or two.

I got up at a folk club in North London where Alex was that evening's guest, and sang 'Maggie's Waddin'. Alex was much taken with 'Maggie'. He asked me to come and sing it again at his next gig, after midnight that same night in the Partisan coffee house in Soho, where one of the resident singers was a very youthful Long John Baldry.

I saw Alex again years later in Glasgow. He was singing in one of our concert halls. The Ian Campbell Folk Group were on, so was another noted performer whose identity evades me. She had long lank hair, wore a long lank dress, sang long lank ballads, and her personality was short on joie d'existence. Shall we call her Alanka?

Anyway, Alex was in some wise filling the role of compere. At one point he complained about who was getting paid what. 'Here's The Campbell group—they all arrived in a Jaguar. Here's Alanka—she arrived in a Jaguar. And here's me—with the seat hanging out of my jeans.' He turned around, and in the days long before designer shredded denims his native flesh was indeed on view.

The last time I saw him was on Glasgow Green in the early 80s, at the Glasgow International Folk Festival. Alex sat beside me to talk to some friends. His vocal chords were so damaged he could not sing any more.

NANCY WHISKY

Although a couple of hundred years ago Calton was a separate village from Glasgow, now it's at the heart of the East End.

In *The Singing Island*, a superb collection of folksongs, Ewan MacColl and Peggy Seeger note that this version of the song is 'From the singing of Hughie Martin of Shettleston, Glasgow, who claims that MacColl's father wrote the tune.' The tune I print is in turn a variation on MacColl's father's tune.

Someone—I don't know who—has more recently turned the bouncy 2/4 tune which I print here into a 3/4 time which gives it a lovely swing—like heavy petticoats swinging in a polka.

NANCY WHISKY

I'm a wea-ver, a Cal-ton wea-ver. I'm a rash and a rov-ing blade. I've got sil-ler in my poo-ches,

I'll gang fol-low the ro-ving trade. CHORUS Whis- ky, Whis-ky, Nan-cy Whis-ky. Whis- ky, whis-ky Nan- cy O.

I cam in by Glesga city.
Nancy Whisky I chanced to smell.
I gaed in, sat doon beside her.
Seven years I lo'ed her well.

The mair I kissed her the mair I lo'ed her.
The mair I kissed her the mair she smiled.
I forgot my mither's teaching.
Nancy soon had me beguiled.

I woke up early in the morning
To slake my drouth it was my need.
I tried to rise but I wasnae able.
Nancy had me by the heid.

'Come landlady, what's the lawin'?
Tell me what there is to pay?'
'Fifteen shillings is the reckoning.
Pay me now and go away.'

I went oot by Glesga city.
Nancy Whisky I chanced to smell.
I gaed in, drank four and sixpence.
All that was left was a crooked scale.

I'll gang back to the Calton weaving.
I'll surely mak the shuttles fly.
I'll mak mair at the Calton weaving
Than ever I did in a roving wey.

Come all ye weavers, Calton weavers.
All ye weavers where e'er ye be.
Beware of whisky, Nancy Whisky.
She'll ruin you as she ruined me.

'Come alang wi' me if you want to see'

The people's history in the People's Palace

Dick Gaughan—THE FREEDOM COME-ALL-YE
Alex Jamieson—PEOPLE'S PALACE
John McCreadie—DOOMSDAY IN THE
AFTERNOON
Ewan MacColl—JAMIE FOYERS
Robin Hall—ROTHESAY-O
Ray Fisher—SHIFT AND SPIN
Freddie Anderson—BONNYMUIR

'COME ALANG WI' ME IF YOU WANT TO SEE'

I sit here resisting temptation.

I want to help you understand about the songs I've put into this section. Why they give a taste of Glasgow's rich history. What other songs I might have used and what they would have shown you. Some of the slices of Glasgow's past that deserve to have new songs written about them.

But there has been a whole book written just about the People's Palace and Glasgow Green. Another called *Auld Hawkie* about the street characters of Glasgow's past.

Enough books have been published on Glasgow's history in recent years to sink the Carrick.

I'll try to confine myself to subjects that I can link songs to.

The Glasgow International Folk Festival has a strong connection with the Green, and the Palace in particular. Concerts, dancing displays, meetings of music enthusiasts—all have a home in the Palace. As do the famous 'banana boots' worn by Billy Connolly. In the Palace's display for 1990 there is what is asserted to be the original Stone of Destiny—the real 'Wee Magic Stane'.

Out on the Green political song is and was part of political action. Look at Hamish Henderson's 'John MacLean March'. Adam McNaughtan wrote 'We Will Not Have A Motorway' to oppose a threat to the Green, as Alex Jamieson's 'Palace' song arose from a threat to the place.

In 1990 the Mayday celebrations were on the Green. Singers included Dick Gaughan and Billy Bragg who sang a duet of 'The Red Flag' to its original tune—the Jacobite song 'The White Cockade'. In other years Matt McGinn's song 'We'll Have A Mayday Then' has been used.

Non-political songs linked to the Green include 'Glasgow Fair', in which the young hero regrets that he has recently 'trysted wi Maggie M'Vicar'. And 'Bonny Glasgow Green' in which a visiting tradesman praises the looks of one of the young washerwomen of the Green and entices her away with him to Aberdeen.

There was a lot of this sort of thing about. Jimmy McBeath's 'Roving Baker', who talks a lass into an alehouse and causes her to lose her Feeing Time. The 'Dundee Weaver' girl who was courted by a Glesga fella who stole her thingummyjig awa on the banks of the Kelvinhaugh. The brisk and braw Highland lad who stole away 'Glasgow Peggy'.

'Jock Hawk' has a famous 'Adventure In Glasgow'. He meets a lass who wanders with him 'up Jamaica Street an roon the Broomielaw', and into a tavern where the sailor lads and their girls welcome him. They all have a fine time, then everyone goes out suddenly leaving Jock to pay the bill for the whole night's drinking. The landlord strips him of possessions and most of his clothing.

> Ah cam intae this world o woe sae naked and sae bare.
> Ah'll gang hame the same frae Glesga, and ah'll never come back nae mair.

126

But the ploughman gets his revenge in a song called 'The Bonny Wee Lassie That Never Said No'. The wee lassie gets drunk, and when she asks him for money, he steals from her instead.

There seems to be some sort of moral here.

Well known old street characters have been revived in Glasgow song.

Auld Hawkie was a famous singer and seller of ballads. Freddie Anderson wrote about him -

> O gather round and I'll tell you my tale
> O' the times I was jovial an' hearty an' hale,
> But this prick-the-louse tailor's attention was such
> That I limp round the town on this tattered auld crutch.

Another modern songwriter whose name is mislaid wrote about the same man -

> Gather round all you fine folk, in your silks and your laces.
> Gather round here and listen to me.
> I was the last man who spoke to the prisoner
> Before he was hung on yon auld gallows tree.

Funny how both writers chose the same opening. Both of them have written songs about another character, Hirstlin Kate, who had lost the use of her legs altogether.

The unknown writer begins, to a tune from Newfoundland,

> Kate, you're bonny, Kate you're sweet.
> It's a shame you canny use yer feet
> As you go bauchlin up the street,
> Hirstlin on yer way-oh.

While Freddie says

> See Hirstlin' Kate o' the town
> On her brushes go sweepin' round,
> Some heads may be high
> Peerin' into the sky,
> But Katie's is fixed on the ground.

There are of course many songs about the trades of Glasgow. Some of the many shipyard songs I've used elsewhere.

'Bonnymuir', 'Shift And Spin' and 'Nancy Whisky' all link the weavers of Glasgow. Archie Fisher made a fine reworking of 'The Factory Maid'

> I'm a handloom weaver to my trade.
> Long time I've courted a factory maid,
> And if I could her fine favour win
> I'd stand beside her and I'd weave by steam.
> For many years now I have plied my skill ·
> By my own fireside, long before the mill.
> I wove fine linen, and the silks of fame
> But the pitching shuttle sings my lassie's name.
> The daisy portion of my father's age
> Is withered now to a meagre wage.
> The dark mill factories of Anderstown
> Have brought the prices, and the weavers, down.

Reaching a little from the city, perhaps the finest lament for the victims of the coal industry, 'The Blantyre Explosion', begins

> By Clyde's bonny banks as I sadly did wander.
> Among the pit heaps as evening drew nigh.

Alasdair Robertson's modern reworking of the story says

> This was the worst disaster
> Since Scottish industry began
> At a mine producing faster
> Than most of the others in the land.
> While mothers, wives and daughters
> Lost their men in the smoke and fire,
> The beggers and street hawkers
> Were the only ones who gained from High Blantyre.
> And it might have been the owner's greed,
> Or the manager's neglect,
> Or the nation's drive for the power we need,
> Or Johnny Murphy's cigarette.

Johnny Murphy and many another Irishman came over for employment. One branch of my family were Irish experts in sinking pit shafts who came and travelled around central Scotland opening up new pits.

Among the people flooding into Glasgow, many were dispossessed Highlanders. A song written for the show about Glasgow which was performed in its twin town of Nurnberg in 1985 records Clearances in Glen Calvie in Sutherland in 1846.

> I am come tae the Lowlands low, ochone, ochone machree.
> Withoot a penny in my pouch tae buy tobacco wi.
> It wisna so on the Hieland hills before Gillanders came
> Tae pit us oot o Calvie Glen, and set fire tae oor hames.
> I curse the factor and the laird, that brought the muckle sheep.
> The law gives them the power to wound but they'll not mak me weep.

The Highland influence is still strong in Glasgow singing.

As is the Irish. When I glanced at a book of Ulster songs I found 'The Glasgow Barber' and 'The Lass From Glasgow Town'.

Travelling agricultural workers came from Ireland, some came for the chance of advancement in the big city, and it was easy to catch a night boat into the Broomielaw.

> I shipped aboard a cattle boat down at Belfast Pier.
> It rambled through the Firth of Clyde and then it dumped me here.
> I have a cousin that'll help, if I can track him down.
> So it's goodbye to old Ireland, and hullo Glasgow Town.
> (To the Irish tune 'Slieve Gallon Braes')

The terrible famine years of the 1840s when the potato crops failed brought many people to Glasgow from the Highlands of Scotland and from Ireland.

> The taters they grew smaller, then they wouldn't grow at all.
> We fed ourselves on acorn bread, or turned to face the wall.
> But still our English landlords demanded 'money down!'
> So it's goodbye to old Ireland, and hullo Glasgow Town.

And waves of political struggle resulted in Irishmen needing a hideyhole in the backcourt tenements of Glasgow.

> We did our best to fight them but the Ribbon Boys were beat.
> And Fighting Dan O'Connell was the first to cry 'defeat'!
> Once more we kneel in fealty to the forces of the crown.
> So it's goodbye to old Ireland, and hullo Glasgow Town.
> I'll set for you a riddle, you may solve it as you please.
> Which is better—stand and die, or live upon your knees?
> Keep your answer for yourself, I've an answer found,
> And it's goodbye to old Ireland and hullo Glasgow Town.

E

Such new Glaswegians brought with them a streak of radical politics, a questioning of traditional values, a rich sense of language and turns of phrase that helped to build the identity of the city.

A city that was growing richer.

> Crail,Weems and Kirkcaldy are famous for haddies.
> Stirling may boast of her salmon so fine.
> Aberdeen of her crabs, cockles, lobsters and speldings
> But the fat Glasgow Magistrate swims in Loch Fyne.
> There's eggs in the Higate and tripe in the Briggate.
> In King Street there's flesh and there's kale in it too.
> In Stockwell there's a wealth o baith meal and potatoes
> And Trongate will fit ye wi hats and wi shoes.
> (To the tune of 'Haste To The Wedding')

But the wealth was always reserved for the few. The hated factors who collected rent on behalf of absentee landlords caught the brunt of public opinion. When rent increases were outrageous rent strikes were organised. A Glasgow one led by women during World War One resulted in Government legislation to stop rent profiteering.

> Hard up, kick the can, Glasgow factors have a plan.
> They'll be sorry they began when they see the rent strike.
> Hard up, pockets out, show them what it's all about.
> Raise yer banner, raise the shout—'We support the rent strike'.
> Hard up, kick the ba, time the landlords had a fa.
> Aa fur one and one fur aa, come and join the rent strike.
> (To the tune of 'Katie Bairdie')

> Tell yer boss when you go back tae stick his summons in his haversack.
> Tell his nibs he's no on, we live here and we're no gaun.
> No more rent for profiteers, no more rent—no bloody fear!
> He can blaw and raise a fuss, he'll get no more rent from us.
> (To the tune of 'I'll Tell My Ma')

Councillors were caught between two positions on the rent strikes, but Glasgow councillors have always had a hard life.

As a song above shows, an old nickname for the Loch Fyne herring was 'A Glasgow Magistrate', suggesting that the worthies of the local court were rather plump and oily.

On the other side, the following shows real sympathy for the pressures put on the public servant. Perhaps.

As ah came doon the Broomielaw ah met a bonnie lass
Who stopped right in front of me and wouldny let me pass.
Says she 'Are you the Provost? Ma wean's near twelve month old.
Ah'll tak a pound as soon as ye can, ah'm awful wet an cold.'
As ah cam in by Brigton Cross ah met an auld auld man
Who stopped, an puttin on his specs, keenly me did scan.
Said he, 'Are ye a cooncillor, ah'm wan o heaven's poor.
Ah'll tak some coals an whiskey, an twa three sacks o floor.'
As ah came up Jamaica Street ah met a bonny laddie
Who looked me up and doon and said 'Yer awful like ma daddy.
What wy's it on the Sabbath we starve in Rouken Glen?
An whiles they houk the streets up, then fill the holes again?'
(To the tune 'The Garden Where The Praties Grow')

Much crueler is the old story of the Glasgow councillor at the time of the great Empire Exhibition. The exhibition was to be in Kelvingrove Park, and officials had suggested a number of gondolas be imported from Venice to ply the River Kelvin for hire.

'Naw, naw,' said the defender of the public purse. 'Let's just import two gondolas, and let them breed!'

A good story is preferable to ten pages of historical facts.

DICK GAUGHAN

Dick is one of Leith's finest, a renowned singer and champion of Scots song old and new, a songwriter of strength and conviction.

He sang this song on the big stage on Glasgow Green, May Sunday, 1990, the hundredth anniversary of Mayday as a people's holiday.

Dick introduced it by saying 'I've been singing this song a long time to try and get people to think of adopting it as a Scottish anthem. Because apart from anything else it does not once mention England or the English.

'It talks about the human race, and the fact that although there are only five million of us and we are just a wee country we should be proud to be equal partners in the human race with everyone else.'

THE FREEDOM COME-ALL-YE

Hamish Henderson's magnificent song is indeed Scotland's alternative national anthem for many people who find 'Flower Of Scotland' depressing and negative.

However, Hamish hopes it never becomes an 'official' anthem ; part of its strength he feels lies in the fact that it is alternative. Among the singers who have adopted it into their repertoire are Pete Seeger and the late Luke Kelly of the Dubliners. But Dick Gaughan is generally agreed to be its finest exponent.

Hamish sings it himself on the album *Freedom Come-All-Ye* (Scottish Folk Bands For Ethiopia).

The song was written for Scottish CND marchers in 1960—one of the songs coaxed out of writers by Morris Blythman.

The tune is called 'The Bloody Fields Of Flanders', a First World War pipe tune which Hamish first heard played on the Anzio beachhead by Pipie Tom Smith of the 6th Gordons (Banffshire battalion). Two other magnificent songs by Hamish came from the Italian campaign—'The Banks Of Sicily' and 'D Day Dodgers'.

Hamish notes that the 'Flanders' tune itself stems from the Perthshire folksong 'Busk Busk Bonnie Lassie'. The MacLean of the lyrics is of course John MacLean—see 'The John MacLean March'.

132

THE FREEDOM COME-ALL-YE

Roch the wind in the clear day's daw-in', blaws the cloods heel-ster gow-dy ow'r the bay. But there's mair nor a roch wind blaw-in' through the great glen o' the warld the day. It's a thocht that will gar oor rot-tans - a' they rogues that gang gal fresh and gay-lus tak' the road an' seek ith-er loan-ins for their ill ploys tae sport an' play.

Nae mair will the bonnie callants
Mairch tae war, when oor braggarts crousely craw,
Nor wee weans frae pit-heid an' clachan
Mourn the ships sailin' doon the Broomielaw.
Broken faimlies in lands we've herriet
Will curse Scotland the Brave nae mair, nae mair;
Black an' white, ane til ither mairriet
Mak' the vile barracks o' their majsters bare.

O come all ye at hame wi freedom,
Never heed whit the hoodies croak for doom,
In your hoose a' the bairns o' Adam
Can find breid, barley bree an' painted room.
When MacLean meets wi's freens in Springburn
A' the roses an' geans will turn tae bloom.
And a black boy frae yont Nyanga
Dings the fell gallows o' the burghers doon.

Words by Hamish Henderson
Music 'The Bloody Fields Of Flanders'

ALEX JAMIESON

Alex dropped me a line—and a cassette crammed with good songs—after a newspaper item about this book.

His song about The People's Palace had already caught my eye, on the album called *The Patter*.

His tape showed that he is an accordionist, and can write good songs on such subjects as his walking stick and his local Community Council.

I asked him to tell me more.

'There's an old Chinese proverb which goes 'The longest journey in the world begins with the first step'. The first belated step on the song-writing trail for Alexander Jamieson began with a song which was kindly passed through Jimmie Macgregor to Alastair McDonald who subsequently recorded it, called 'No Trident No!' which requires no further definition.

'Alastair, who has helped me enormously to get established as a writer, then went on to record my next song, 'The People's Palace'.'

THE PEOPLE'S PALACE

'The story about this song really began way back when I was a wee laddie in Glengarnock, Ayrshire, and although not a Glaswegian (all my folk on Dad's side were) I was always fascinated by the excitement of Glasgow, especially the boats at the Broomielaw, the horses and carts, the beloved old tramcars.

'My Uncle Josh took me to the People's Palace one day, which I never forgot - particularly the planetarium, a great feature of the Palace at that time. The next occasion I visited it was about 1985. All the memories came flooding back and I was hooked again, as well as being saddened by the obvious neglect which had been taking place.

'Then I heard about the Friends Of The People's Palace and their heroic struggle to save the place, I couldn't contain my emotions, and found myself writing the song the same night. Within weeks Ali McDonald had recorded it.'

134

THE PEOPLE'S PALACE

CHORUS Come a-lang wi' me if ye want tae see the pa-lace o' the peo-ple. Stan-din a-lone in the red sand-stone wi' a big high dome and stee-ple. The place vi-brates wi' Gles-ga greats, for the wor-king man they spoke. Be you grave or gal-lus, take a trip tae the pal-ace that be-longs tae the Gles-ga folk. As I went wal-kin' wi' the weans and my wee wi-fey, A-lice, I telt a stran-ger I'd just met a-boot my east-ern pa-lace. Says he tae me "That just can't be, you're not a king, old bean." But I proved him wrang wi' the words o' a sang at a place called the Glas-gow Green.

re were galleries great in the year '98
the west end o' the city.
vingrove was a treasure trove
there just remained one pity.
as a horse drawn tram or a walk wi' a pram.
the day that they were released
e the hassle and the malice, wi' the building o' a Palace
the folk that were broke in the east.

w you'll learn o' Glesga if you seek
w Gaelic the Dear Green Place is.
've a coat of arms that's quite unique
history proudly traces.
Mungo is the Patron Saint, depicted you can see 'im.
this and more you will find in store
the old P.P. museum.

So come wi' me and we'll go and see
This winter garden treasure
And let's spare a thought for yon fine lot
Who fought to save our pleasure.
Let's never take for granted this old structure fair and fine.
It's standin' there for us all to share.
'Cause the Palace is yours and mine!

Words and music by Alex Jamieson

JOHN MCCREADIE

A member of the group Diggery Venn and a strong solo singer.
His version of John Martyn's 'Dont You Go My Son' has startled many an audience, and impressed more than one worldweary BBC engineer.
His political songwriting is also impressive.

> As I went out by Cardowan bings I heard a young man say
> Once I was a miner but they've ta'en my job away.
> I used to work the coalface of that mine ower the field.
> We always made our quota, we always got good yield.
> But a man came from America, I curse him to this day.
> McGregor rationalised me and he's ta'en my job away.

DOOMSDAY IN THE AFTERNOON

John's local Milngavie paper reported meetings to protest council plans for a local campsite for travelling people.

John linked this to stories told by traveller Belle Stewart of Blairgowrie about prejudice she had encountered. The title comes from Belle's answer to the question 'When will the travellers stop moving?'

When you think about travellers, remember that there are several different groups travelling the roads of Scotland. There are the Romany descendants of nomadic North Indian metal-working tribes who travelled across Europe to reach Scotland four or five hundred years ago. They claimed to have come from Egypt, so were called Egyptians or Gypsies for short.

There were broken clans from the 1745 Rebellion, and families forced from their homes in the glens of Sutherland and elsewhere in the North and West during the 19th Century Clearances, and freed serfs from much earlier times.

Then there are the travelling Show people, who claim a very different descent.

All of these groups occasionally make their home on vacant sites in Glasgow. One part of Shettleston is labelled on the map Little Egypt.

In their long visit the travellers have experienced much hostility from the settled peoples, who must themselves at some earlier date have been travellers in order to arrive here.

And as the travellers picked over the leavings of the earlier arrivals to find and salvage metal, they also found and preserved songs and stories, so that much of Scotland's heritage of song has been recovered by folklorists from traveller singers like Jeannie Robertson and the Stewarts of Blair.

DOOMSDAY IN THE AFTERNOON

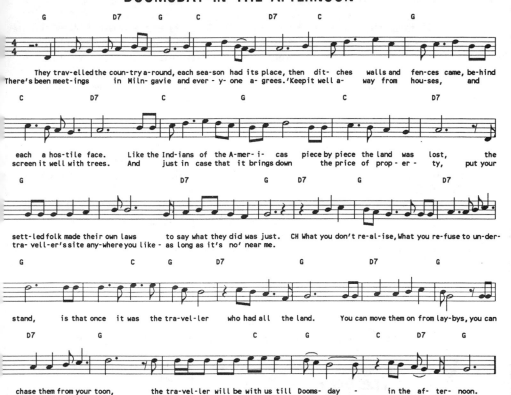

They trav-elled the coun-try a-round, each sea-son had its place, then dit- ches walls and fen-ces came, be-hind
There's been meet-ings in Miln- gavie and ever - y- one a- grees. 'Keep it well a- way from hou-ses, and

each a hos-tile face. Like the Ind-ians of the A-mer- i- cas piece by piece the land was lost, the
screen it well with trees. And just in case that it brings down the price of prop - er - ty, put your

sett-led folk made their own laws to say what they did was just. CH What you don't re-al-ise, What you re-fuse to un-der-
tra- vell-er's site any-where you like - as long as it's no' near me.

stand, is that once it was the tra-vel-ler who had all the land. You can move them on from lay-bys, you can

chase them from your toon, the tra-vel-ler will be with us till Dooms- day - in the af- ter- noon.

The Queen welcomed Belle at the Palace, but in her local she can't get a hauf.
'For we don't serve dirty tinks in here, we soon see that lot off.'
And in her local supermarket she heard two women say,
'I don't know what the Queen was thinking, ge'ing a tink a medal onyway.'

The travellers were at Auschwitz, there were travellers at Belsen too.
The Nazis treated the traveller the same way as the Jew.
But history turns a blind eye and remembers what it will.
For the travelling people there is no Israel.

Words and music by John McCreadie
Published by Bonskeid Music.

137

EWAN MACCOLL

If Hamish Henderson is the Grand Old Man of the Scottish Folk Revival, Ewan MacColl was the key person in the British Folk Revival - singer, song collector and songwriter, innovator and traditionalist, playwright and documentor.

In 1953 he wrote 'Given the same broadcasting facilities as Jazz and Swing it is not outside the realms of possibility that in a few years' time the young people of Glasgow and Edinburgh might come to prefer their own musical idiom to the idiom of Bing Crosby and Frank Sinatra.'

As a songwriter his work ranges from 'Dirty Old Town' to 'The First Time Ever I saw Your Face', from 'Shoals Of Herring' to 'Go Down You Murderers'. Many of his songs have the same time-defying qualities as any Big Ballad.

The Radio Ballad format that he created with the involvement of his wife, Peggy Seeger, and producer Charles Parker transformed the use of actuality speech in radio, and also produced many of his finest songs.

His work as a playwright with Theatre Workshop and with BBC Radio was seminal. He and Peggy taught young singers and songwriters, and collected old songs from travelling people.

 A Scot by ancestry and adoption, his singing visits to Glasgow in the 1950s helped give us a notion of folk music as a living force not dependent on teachers, academics or concert promoters. He is sorely missed, but his influence will live on.

JAMIE FOYERS

The first verse and the tune are 175 years old, about a Perthshire militiaman dying in Spain in the Peninsular wars against Napoleon.

Ewan MacColl learned the old song from his mother's singing, and wrote a new version during the Spanish Civil War, marking the many men who went from Clydeside to fight on the side of the Republicans in Spain.

'Jamie Foyers' is a much loved song in Scotland. I am working on a recorded history of Scottish political songs. I have had more offers by singers to record 'Jamie Foyers' than any other song—except of course for 'The Freedom Come-All-Ye'.

Jimmie Macgregor recalls that when he and Robin Hall were presenting the TV *White Heather Club* they did one programme on the deck of the newly built QE2, in which Roddy McMillan sang 'Jamie Foyers' and reduced a crowd of a thousand riveters and apprentices to silence!

JAMIE FOYERS

Far dis-tant, far dis-tant, lies Foy-ers the brave, no tomb-stone me- mo- ri-al shall hal-low his grave

His bones they are scat-tered on the rude soil of Spain, for young Ja- mie Foy-ers in bat- tle lies slain.

He's gane frae the shipyard that stands on the Clyde,
His hammer is silent, his tools laid aside.
To the wide Ebro river young Foyers has gane.
To fecht by the side o' the people of Spain.

There wasna his equal at work or at play,
He was strang in the union till his dying day;
He was grand at the fitba', at the dance he was braw,
O, young Jamie Foyers was the flower o' them a'.

He cam' frae the shipyard, took aff his working-claes.
O, I mind that time weel in the lang summer days;
He said, 'Fare ye weel, lassie, I'll come back again,'
But young Jamie Foyers in battle was slain.

In the fecht for Belchite he was aye to the fore.
He focht at Gandesa till he couldna fecht more;
He lay owre his machine-gun wi' a bullet in his brain.
And young Jamie Foyers in battle was slain.

Words by Ewan MacColl
Published by Harmony Music

ROBIN HALL

Archie Fisher says Robin was 'The first straight ballad singer I'd ever come across. He had a God-given voice.'

Robin was another who attended Allan Glen's and was influenced by Morris Blythman. His first recordings had such a pleasant light touch it is small wonder his recorded versions of songs became the revival favourites and drove other local variants out.

It was Robin's recording of 'The Bleacher Lassie Of Kelvinhaugh' that became well-known and turned John MacDonald's version into 'the old way of the song'.

Then Robin joined with Jimmie Macgregor. (See Jimmie Macgregor for details of their joint career.)

The Reivers were home-grown and home-nurtured Scottish, but Robin and Jimmie were successful at a national level—alongside but more successful than Rory & Alex McEwan, and Cy Grant.

At one point Robin and Jimmie joined with Shirley Bland and Leon Rosselson to make an excellent group called The Galliards.

Both Robin and Jimmie have latterly made their careers back in Scotland on BBC Radio.

ROTHESAY-O

The Galliards recorded a version of this epic story of a doon the watter jaunt, but I recall Robin singing it solo many years ago in Glasgow—maybe at Allan Glen's—with a lilt that showed the joyous ballad nature of the song and was light years away from the heavy thumping it often got and still gets from guitar wallopers.

This printed version is not the only way of the song.

A few years ago I was standing outside the bar on Wemyss Bay Pier, waiting for the ferry over to Rothesay. I heard a song being lifted inside—this one, but with substantially different words. Was it older or newer?

Why didn't I go inside and find out? Just shy. I'd never have made a good folk-song collector.

ROTHESAY-O

One Hog-man-ay at the Gles- ga Fair there was me ma-sel an sev-er- al mair, we aa set off tae hae a terr and
CHORUS Durrum a doo a dum a day Durrum a doo a dad- dy O. Durrum a doo a dum a day The

spend the day in Rothe-say-O. We wan-dered doon the Broom-ie-law thro wind and rain, and sleet and snaw, and at
day we went to Rothe-say-O.

for- ty mee-nits ef- ter twa we got the length o Rothe- say- O.

A sodger lad ca'd Ru'glen Wull wha's regiment's lying at Barnhill
Went aff wi a tanner tae buy a gill in a public hoose in Rothesay-O.
Says he 'Be God, I'd like tae sing.' Says I 'Ye'll dae nae sich a thing.'
He says 'Clear the flair and mak a ring and ah'll kill yez aa in Rothesay-O.'

In search o' ludgins we did slide, tae find a place whaur we could bide.
There was eichty-four o us inside a single-end in Rothesay-O.
We aa lay doon tae tak oor ease when one o the boys began tae sneeze.
An' he waukened half a million fleas that et us alive in Rothesay-O.

Some were bees and some were bugs, and some had feet like dyers' clugs.
They sat on the bed and they cockit their lugs and cried 'Hurrah for Rothesay-O'.
Says I 'I think we should elope', so we went an jined the Band o Hope.
But the polis widny let us stop anither oor in Rothesay-O.

RAY FISHER

All the Fisher family women are impressive—Mrs Fisher, Audrey, Joyce, Cindy and Cilla. But Ray is the queen of them all.

According to her brother Archie she 'started as a vamp, singing traditional jazz. She'd go out in a white sheath dress singing 'How I Hate A Man Like You'.'

Then she was the strong-voiced half of RayanArchie on STV in the early 60s.

She has recorded criminally few times—because she doesn't enjoy it.

I sent her this song and heard nothing for years. Then the phone rang. Marie Dufresne of Brunswick, Maine, was calling from the US of A. She had learned the song from Ray, and wanted to record it.

When later I met up with Ray she told me she had given the words to a number of singers, but with the proviso 'Now promise that you won't record it until I've done so myself'.

This is great. Nothing nicer for a songwriter than to hear that singers want the words to your song.

There's just one problem. Ray, as is the way with singers, has individualised the song. She's changed the tempo, amended the tune, altered the mood and edited the words. That's all right, I'm working in the folk song idiom, where you take it for granted that singers will change songs.

But since it is her version, not mine, that most people have heard, my version has become the 'wrong' one.

SHIFT AND SPIN

The chorus of this song was written for a local history project in Paisley, Renfrewshire, recording the history of workers in the Paisley thread mills.

Then, at the urging of Danny Kyle verses were added to be sung by Alan Tall and Lillian Cattigan in a show on the history of Glasgow. This show was specially written in three languages—German, English and Glesga—to be performed in Glasgow's twin city of Nurnberg in 1985 as a part of the official twinning events.

Later I reworked the verses a little so I could sing it solo. So there are a couple of varying versions around.

This is my own favourite.

142

SHIFT AND SPIN

Keep yer bob- bins run- nin ea- sy, Show ye're gal- lus, bright and bree- zy,
JS Shift and spin, warp and twine, Ma- king thread coarse and fine,

Wai-- tin till Prince Char- min sees ye, Wor- kin in the mill.
Drea- min o yer va- len- tine, Wor- kin in the mill.

Oil yer runners, mend yer thread,
Do yer best until ye're dead.
Wish ye were a wife instead o
Workin in the mill.

Used to dream you'd be the rage,
Smilin on the fashion page.
Never dreamt you'd be a wage slave
Workin in the mill.

Used to think that life was kind.
No it isn't—never mind
Maybe some day love will find you
Workin in the mill.

He loves you not? So what?
Do the best with what you've got.
Win your pay, spin yer cotton,
Workin in the mill.

Words and music by Ewan McVicar
Published by Gallus Music

FREDDIE ANDERSON

An adopted son of Glasgow, another Irishman, from Co Monaghan in Ulster.

Freddie has been writing and pleasing audiences for many years. His lyric style derives in part from the best of folk song, and Hamish Henderson recently described his work as belonging to 'a long line of courageous radical poets whose most famous members include Byron and Burns—not forgetting Woody Guthrie'.

Freddie's novel *Oiney Hoy* was recently published to glowing reviews, and he has won more than one Festival Fringe First award for his playwriting.

He is an upholder of the broadsheet and flyting tradition. In addition to editing the Scotia Bar newspaper for some years, he would regularly tour the pub to distribute cyclostyled copies of a song he'd just written in praise or blame of someone in the local or international news.

Freddie wrote one of the best of the Anti-Polaris songs, 'The Polis O Argyll', to the Irish tune 'Johnson's Motor Car'.

> These worthy sons of Robert Peel are trained to keep the law,
> And any danger they'll confront, providin it is sma.
> In naval operations they specialise in style,
> But the Holy Loch proved quite a shock to the polis o Argyll.

The first time I entered the Scotia Bar, it was a quiet early evening. I went in and sat in the Wee Back Room. Freddie looked across at me and said 'Hullo. You look like a man that could sing a song.'

Freddie has friends all round the globe, and enemies very few.

BONNYMUIR (aka CALTON WEAVER LADS)

Freddie is an enthusiast for the history of Glasgow. He contributed the poems for the book *Auld Hawkie* about Glasgow street characters, and has written a play about Glasgow bairn Wee Willy Winkie.

His poem 'Bonnymuir', subtitled 'A Tribute to the Brave Men of 1820', was printed in a recent collection of his work, *At Glasgow Cross and other poems*.

Freddie's poem has been set by Edinburgh singer, songwriter and activist John Greig to a widely-used tune. John's variant derives from 'The Smashing Of The Van', an account of the rescue of an Irish prisoner from a police van in Glasgow's High Street in 1921.

BONNYMUIR

I am a Cal-ton wea-ver lad and sim- ple is my plea.
We tried to make a un- ion then, our scan-ty rights de-fend;

Not to be tied for- ev- er to four
the cot-ton and to - bac-co lairds its

posts of pov-er -ty; the grim dark days o' Cas-tle-reagh have set-tled with their blight,
ru- in did in- tend: they hir-ed an in-for - mer - Rich-mond was his name,

though the sun shines down on Glas - gow town, it seems e - ter - nal night.
and bribed with gold our Cause he sold to mis- er - y and shame.

'Twas early in the April and the Springtime o' the year.
As I went down the Ladywell, a great crowd did appear;
They read a notice on the wall: Tae Arms! Tae Arms! it cried.
'Twas there that Andra Hardy stood and Tyranny defied.

As we went up by Carronside, ah, what a sad, brave sight.
A little band o' marching men to match a nation's might:
With only pikes and staves half-armed, a weavers' poor platoon.
But hearts so brave to stand the waves of sabre and dragoon.

Oh, there's dancing in the Tontine now, the bells toll our defeat,
And the rich who cowered with their gear now strut the open street,
And saintly ministers thank God how he preserved the State.
Gave it relief though bowed with grief the poor o' Gallowgate.

As we came in by Stirling, you'd hear the clanking chain.
The poor gaunt Calton weaver lads at Bonnymuir were taken;
They hanged two in the castle, Baird and Hardy were their names:
Though turned to mould is Richmond's gold, untarnished lives their fame!

The remainder were in irons clamped and banished o'er the waves.
Neath the Southern Star in a land afar, you'll find their patriot graves,
And Jamie Wilson o' Strathaven Vale, a man advanced in years.
Nigh Glasgow Cross his life he lost among the people's tears.

Farewell bold Calton weaver lads! On Castlereagh my curse!
His end in bloody suicide had murder as its source;
Farewell brave lads o' Glasgow who died your lands to save!
Auld Scotia's rose in blossom grows aboon the weavers' grave.

Words by Freddie Anderson
Music 'The Smashing Of The Van'

145

'My place and habitation'

By Clyde's bonnie banks

Ian Davison—GOING HOME TO GLASGOW
Big Mick Broderick—BALLAD OF THE Q4
Billy Connolly—SALTCOATS AT THE FAIR
Paul Joses—MY SONG OF THE CLYDE
Jim Brown—THE WAVERLEY POLKA
Bill McVicar—WHA SAW THE 42ND and
        TODAY IS HOGMANAY
Cy Laurie—JAMIE RAEBURN

'MY PLACE AND HABITATION'

We heard the hooters from the big boats on the Clyde just before 'the bells' at midnight each Hogmanay in the 1950s when—glasses in hands—we opened our front door in Balshagray Avenue facing across to Victoria Park and stood there to 'let the New Year in'.

Early hooters had already started by five minutes to midnight,

the blast of a freighter's horn

and new ones would begin to bellow as late as five minutes into the year— according to the timekeeping of our radio. (This was in the days before events were synchronised by reference to the television set. Before the English had found out from television about Hogmanay.)

Since I'd learned at school that it was the pinpoint accuracy of their chronometers which allowed these great ships to navigate their way safely around the globe, I was a little alarmed to think that some of their timepieces disagreed by as much as ten minutes. This was surely enough to cause them to miss some islands altogether, and lead to impressive crashes in narrow straits off Java or Tierra Del Fuego.

Many a year later, I proposed a recreation of Hogmanay On The Clyde as part of the Glasgow Garden Festival. We would rig hooters and fake funnels on top of some of the high rise buildings near the site, plus great noise creators on small row boats. At the sign, New Year would break out, and passing motorists would be asked to join in the row.

We might even get some well known Glasgow composer like John Maxwell Geddes to orchestrate and conduct the event, using light beams in the sky as signals.

Like lots of good ideas, it didn't happen. The idea was more fun than the execution of it, which involved noise control legislation and the finding of money.

Where I live now we still open the door to let the New Year in. In some recent years there has been a hooter or two calling from the Clyde, some years there is silence.

Hogmanay was truly noisy on the river in 1939, when my parents lived in a tenement flat in Balshagray Avenue. They moved north, so I was born in Inverness.

I had a first taste of the connection between the river and the magic of word and song a couple of years before my family moved back to live in Glasgow again.

In 1953 we lived in Dingwall. One night when my father came home weary from work, I greeted him with childish enthusiasm for a poem of Rudyard Kipling I had just found in one of our old leather-bound books.

Dad lit up. He sat on the front room floor beside me and pulled from the bookshelf *Rudyard Kipling's Verse, Inclusive Edition 1885-1918*. The bookplate states it is 'Ex Libris James G McVicar and Agnes D McVicar'. My grandparents.

Dad turned to page 137, and read me the parts he loved best from 'M'Andrew's Hymn', in which an old Glasgow ship's engineer -

> Oh roads we used to tread
> Fra' Maryhill to Pollokshaws—fra' Govan to Parkhead.

reflects on his life and relationship with God, and his understanding of his religion through the workings of the steam engine

> From coupler-flange to spindle-guide I see Thy Hand, O God.

As he stands the night middle watch out on some unnamed sea he reflects on the foolishness of those who regret the loss of the 'romance of sail' and its replacement by prosaic steam. M'Andrew calls for God to send a man like Burns 'to sing the Song o Steam'.

Now of course we mourn the loss of the 'romance of steam' and its replacement by prosaic diesel. There are folksongs in praise of steam engines, Jim Brown hymns The Waverley as Matt McGinn does the Q4.

Yet Paul Joses' Blue Train runs on diesel.

Kipling, a man of his time—of The Empire and The White Man's Burden—was a master word-spinner. He used the ballad form for epic tales, he parodied it, he wrote lyrics sharp as the East Wind about Vikings and Pathans, war and love and trade and life.

In 'M'Andrew's Hymn' his use of Scots vernacular was rather shaky and his version of a Glasgow accent quite vile at times.

But the same criticism is valid for the other major influence on my developing image of Glasgow in the early fifties, *The McFlannels*.

Kipling and the McFlannels gave me a love of the richness of language that all the efforts of my English teachers could not stifle. I merely grew to view school as an irrelevance, particularly after we moved to Glasgow and I encountered the oddball teachers who flourished like orchids in Allan Glen's School.

149

I recently met a luminary from the Old Boys' Association who considered me mentally frail because I had no fond memories of the place. This same worthy has been entrapped in the education system all his life. The prisoner thinks nostalgically of his first Borstal too.

However, glory of glories, one of these oddball Glen's teachers was Morris Blythman. I was already a Lonnie Donegan fan, so when I joined the school Ballads and Blues Club my first instrument was the washboard.

(Let us resist the temptation here to make clever connections between the washboard and the fabled washerwomen of Glasgow Green long ago, treading their employers' clothes and showing the delighted gentlemen passers by that they possessed legs.)

I graduated to guitar and to singing. My version of 'McPherson's Rant' was so spirited that I was dubbed 'the ranting roaring boy' by Ray Fisher.

In the company of the Broomhill Bums I attended a 19 month long party held in a converted laundry and learned much about songs, singing and music.

As related elsewhere I eventually wrote a song called 'Talking Army Blues', which was performed in a Rockall accent. (Rockall is a mid-Atlantic place where nobody lives. Nobody.)

In time I followed my accent to the USA, by way of East Africa, Aden, India and Japan, being in turn a bank manager, a wealthy traveller and a poor but honest guitar teacher.

Then I came home to Glasgow. I have lived here over half my life. This is my home.

The Clyde is my river.

The Clyde is not like the Thames. The Thames turns its back on the city of London—you hardly ever see it.

The Clyde is there catching the eye, broad and proud, with Alasdair Robertson's 'Night lights on the river' as bright gems.

I have been moved on by park rangers for singing on the Clyde Walkway without a permit from the Parks Department, I have performed for small political demos at the same Riverside amphitheatre that held thousands on The Big Day in 1990. I've sung in the Star Club when it was located on the south bank of the Clyde, in the Clyde Valley Stompers Club when it was on the north bank, in the People's Palace on the Green and in many other venues strung along the river.

The Clyde made Glasgow, Glasgow made the Clyde.

The Clyde helped make Glasgow's songs.

Count how many of the songs in this book mention the Clyde and its banks, especially the Broomielaw, where the ships came in.

150

The banana boats, cattle boats, boats crewed by M'Andrew and his like, boats with engines built here, boats launched here—many of my male contemporaries began as shipyard apprentices, to be thrown on the employment scrapheap at the age of 18 when their lowly-paid apprenticeship ended and there were no jobs for them as adults.

Glasgow's tramcars went on the scrapheap too.

For me the tramcars were land boats, and a hurl down the Boulevard was a cheap version of a daytrip to the Kyles. A little bit of Glasgow's heart died with the trams, for that event was like a forecast of the death of the yards.

> The English have Big Ben, that beats every hour.
> The French can swank of their great Eiffel Tower.
> That's all very well if you want to send postcards
> But where else but Clydeside has tramcars and shipyards?
> Tramcars and shipyards, tramcars and shipyards.
> Where would we be without tramcars and shipyards?
> A tramcar'll tak ye where'er ye're inclined
> And rattle yer bones tae wake up yer mind.
> Up tae the school or doon tae the graveyard.
> We wouldn't get far without tramcars and shipyards.
> A shipyard's a place where ye'll aye get a job.
> Ye swing a big hammer tae earn a few bob
> Tae give tae the factor tae mark in yer rent card.
> They're wonderful things, tramcars and shipyards.
> Ah've built a few boats, and they wereny canoes.
> They sail tae America, or Timbuktoo.
> But I ride the trams down the Great Western Boulevard.
> Ah'm happy right here where there's tramcars and shipyards.
> They may not look fancy, but what's that tae me?
> What more dae ye need for the land or the sea?
> The Clyde will be done, the times will have turned hard
> If ever we lose our tramcars and shipyards.
> Tramcars and shipyards, tramcars and shipyards.
> Where will we be without tramcars and shipyards?'
> (To the tune of 'Tatties And Herring')

I wish we had recreated Hogmanay On The Clyde for the Garden Festival. It would have been fun. But it would not have been true. The Clyde is a leisure river, not a working river now. Glasgow seeks its future in leisure and culture, and the warehouses are being turned into residential houses.

Byres Road is more than ever the perch of the culture vultures. But to add to the powerful women of Glasgow, the wee molls, the millionaire maws and the gallus grannies, there are now cool women.

What's that street where you meet cognoscenti?
Well I've went and I've saw and there's plenty.
Guys and dolls, posers all, first-time buyers.
Check the lot, have a stot, on the By-res.
Well there's dancers and chancers and actors.
And Rachmans and Fagins and factors.
Patter merchants and plain bloody liars,
Check the lot, have a stot, on the By-res.
Veggie greens, rice and beans, nuff tae burya.
And tofu it's awfu good furya,
Boi-led crabs, and kebabs, gaun on fi-re.
Check the lot, have a stot, on the By-res.
Up the stairs, there au pairs, and there nurses,
And students wi wee skinny purses,
Aw the chicks huv got six-seiven Highers,
Check the lot, have a stot, on the By-res.
But it's no where ye go fur a lumber.
They're fly and they've aye got yer number.
Macho bores, you'll no score, you're pariahs,
Helluva cool, women rule, on the By-res.
(To the tune 'On The Bayou', by Moyna Gardner, nee Flanigan.)

With new or enforced leisure has come time or pressure to express ourselves. While working on this book I've been sent dozens of new songs of Glasgow.

Of course a few are as wet and windy as a Spring sail doon the watter.

But most are surprisingly well crafted—political, aspirational, humorous, nostalgic, observant, incisive.

Clyde-built and proud of it.

152

IAN DAVISON

Ian was another of the Buchanites from Rutherglen, becoming wellknown with his Ian Davison Folk Four group.

The influence of Norman Buchan at Rutherglen and Morris at Allan Glen's extended further than to singing—it's instructive to consider how many like Ian went on to become teachers! (One of the reasons why several of the songs in this book contain semi-colons, an item only teachers know how to use.)

Ian uses song to advantage in his teaching and his life. He is a trenchant activist in many areas. Ian writes lots of songs. In this morning's post I got two new songs from him—

> How much is that missile in the windae?
> The Trident that turns owre its tail?

and

> Ah'm Peter the Punk. Ah wear trendy junk.
> But ah'm Glesca through and through.
> Ah'm Red, and mean, but ma hair's dyed Green,
> And ma scalp's a loyal Blue.

Our paths had crossed over the years in the Glasgow folk song community. We came together in the SCND Buskers—we found we had independently been working on songs which would harness well known tunes to carry the peace message to sing on demos, to support street stalls, to use in performances.

Ian's songs get right to the point fast.

> We've got nuclear weapons to keep the elephants out.
>
> If Maggie wants to die, fair enough!
>
> It'll be Star Wars for Reagan, and curtains for the world.

He also maintains a regular output of non-campaigning songs, from the gigantic 'Glasgow Budgie' to honest sensual lovesongs to 'The Caves In The Canyons'.

GOING HOME TO GLASGOW

Ian says he wrote this song to a foxtrot beat, but musician Carol Sweeney gave it the Latin touch. The song pinpoints the feeling of warmth we have when home is within sight, and the relief—not related to nervousness about travel—when your feet hit the tarmac or concrete of the town.

154

GOING HOME TO GLASGOW

We're o-ver Beat-tock Sum-mit, we wave a winning fist We're rac-ing down the val-ley where the sil-ver riv-er twists. And now I hear the sound I know I'm Glas-gow bound, The tyres are sing-ing swee-ter as the sun strikes through the mist. CH I'm go-ing home to Glas-gow, its face is on my mind Its laugh is loud and gal-lus, its arms are warm and kind. I need to feel the ground un-der-neath my feet and hear the Glas-gow sounds in the peo-ple that I meet.

The rails are reaching downwards. They point across the plain.
The miles I owe to Glasgow friends are running through my brain.
The restless engine glides towards the valley of the Clyde,
With half-a-thousand homeward bound on the London-Glasgow train.

We soared above the Borders, the white clouds down below.
We caught the winding coastline in the early sunset glow.
We're sliding down the sky, the green hills in our eye.
We swing around the city, and we skim the river low.

Words and music by Ian Davison
Published by Gallus Music

155

BIG MICK BRODERICK

Mick, the man with the bushiest beard this side of Cuba, helped to found and still beats the bodhran with the first Scots folk supergroup, the Whistlebinkies.

Before that he led the Jacobites group.

Big Mick was always a leftover Jacobite, and can sing more songs in praise of Bonny Prince Charlie than any mortal man has a right to know.

I saw him in his full glory one night at Irvine Marymass Folk Festival, when a local dressed him up in full Highland fig, placed him bareback on a black horse, put a claymore and targe into his hands, and led him onto the open stage. Mick brandished his sword and yelled the way his ancestors did to terrify the Lowlanders out of their wits.

> Quod God to the Hielandman, 'Where wilt thou now?'
> 'I will doune in the Lawland, Lord, and there steal a cow.'

A raconteur of ferocious wit and invention, it is no wonder he won the first ever Glasgow Patter Competition, held as part of the Glasgow Folk Festival some years before the book *The Patter* appeared. Get him to tell you the story of the Mickey Mouse clock that saved him from being mugged in Harlem.

Jim Daily, then of the Binkies, remembers Mick with tears in his eyes one night in Germany when the band was being quartered on the floor of the bar where they had performed that evening. There they were, locked in a pub.

But Mick had already had so much to drink earlier in the evening, he couldn't profit from the opportunity!

BALLAD OF THE Q4

Mick helped build the Q4. He served his apprenticeship in John Brown's yard in Clydebank.

I'd always thought that Q4 was somehow linked to the ship's eventual name of the QE2. Mick explains that Q4 was the reference number on the quotation for the job by the Yard.

The older fitters and riveters that Mick knew would boast 'We built yer actual Q4.' When Mick sings Matt's song he makes the last line of the chorus

Make way for yer actual Q4.

THE BALLAD OF THE Q4

The Ma- ry and the Liz-zie they were made right here, but you'll ne-ver see the likes of them I fear.

They were the fin-est on the sil-ver sea. They were built by the hands of men like me.

H Thank you, Dad, for all your skill, but the Clyde is a ri- ver that-'ll no stand still. You

did gey well, but we'll do more, make way for the fin- est of them all, Q 4.

We have an order we'll fulfil
With a touch o' the master and a bit more skill.
Now the backroom boys are under way
And the pens will be rolling till the launching day.

There's Big Tom O'Hara with his burning gear
The plumber and the plater and the engineer
There's young Willie Wylie with his welding rod
They're waiting at the ready for the backroom nod.

We'll burn and cut and shape and bend
We'll be welding and riveting and in the end
When the painter's dabbed his final coat
We'll be launching the finest ever ship afloat.

We've worked and sweated and toiled and now
See the expert's hand from stern to bow
She's ready for the torments o' the sea
She's a credit to the Clyde and you and me.

Words and music by Matt McGinn
Published by Heathside Music

BILLY CONNOLLY

I first knew him as half of The Humblebums, Billy Connolly and Tam Harvey, a good Glasgow folk group.

Billy's introductions to songs got longer and longer. It became clear he was a comic genius, and it seemed a real shame he was too specialised in his humour ever to make it outside Glasgow.

Billy and Tam were joined by Gerry Rafferty, Tam left, then Billy went solo. I hear he's done quite well for himself.

I last spoke to him in the Scotia while he was up for the filming of *The Big Man*. We talked about banjo players we both admired. A few days earlier we'd passed at a literary event when he complimented me on my 'Tam The Bam' song and asked could he sing it.

The answer was 'Yes, please!'

SALTCOATS AT THE FAIR

This was a Humblebums song—I'll attempt to describe the singing style, a slight parody of the classic pub singer style of West Scotland.

All the extra vowels possible are inserted into the song—'Salteeco-aites Ah-Goodeebyee'.

Then you add long-held and lovingly chewed notes and consonants—'did ye' has an extra sss sound through it, achieved by letting the tongue off half its usual work.

Any possible emotion in the song is milked until the udder is wrung out - Billy gets remarkable extra warmth into the child's announcement of the present bought for his mammie.

Long languorous slides are used, and a thick wobble on the top notes, with dramatic gestures—eg the arm sweeping the queue for fish suppers, lifted skyward to show the height of the stack of bread and butter, then gracefully dropped and pointed at the drunks lining the gutters.

I remember singers in the tuning-up room of Glasgow McLellan Galleries telling each other about this epic, and beginning already to doubt they had heard what they had heard.

I have it on a record, but so overlaid with sound effects it doesn't seem funny. You had to be there.

The Fair is of course the Glasgow Fair, the second fortnight of July when Glasgow went to the seaside.

SALTCOATS AT THE FAIR

1) Did ye see the boats gaun doon the wat-tair? Did ye see the bag-gy min-nies scat-tair? Fine well they know what we are af-tair, wi wir nets an wir jee-ly-jaurs in wir hauns. Aa the day we spent at Salt-co-aits, an ra pres-ents that we all go-ait. Ah got a o rock Aun-tie Fan-nie, and a salt dish ma-mmie. stick fur ma fur ma

5) Well, Salt-co-aits good-ee- bye, I hate the smell of yer rot- ten sea-weed. Nev- er a- gain will I see you, Salt- ee- co- aits, good- ee- byee.

2) Aa the day we spent at Saltcoaits,
An ra presents that we all goait.
Ah got a stick o rock fur ma Auntie Fannie,
And a salt dish fur ma mammie.

3) Did ye see thaim queuing fur fish suppairs?
Yer High Fish Tea wi yer bread and yir buttair.
Aa yer drunk men lying in the guttairs.
They were doon at Saltcoats fur the Fair.

4) Says he tae me 'Whit time ur ye leavin, son?'
Says ah tae he 'Boot hauf eleeven, son.
Cos ah'm furra next train up tae Stevenson.
Cos ah don't like Saltcoats at the Fair.'

Words by Billy Connolly
Music 'Come Back To Sorrento'
Published by Heathside Music

159

PAUL JOSES

I dropped into the Star Club one night, to deliver some leaflets about a songwriting competition. The guest singer, his first time in the club as top of the bill although he'd sung there when passing through Glasgow, was an Irishman called Tomas Lynch. I hadn't heard of him.

Tomas stood up and sang a clutch of fine songs including the only almost full version of James Joyce's 'Ballad Of Perse O'Reilly' I've heard. Then he strapped on a set of uillean pipes and played some blistering reels. A fine night.

But between times he caught and held me with a song called 'My Song Of The Clyde' written by a friend of his, a Scot who'd been living in Germany for some years.

Tomas told me that Paul Joses had written a number of songs about Glasgow and the Clyde as a project—I said I would love to hear more.

Six days later the phone rang. Paul Joses was calling from Henglarn. Was I really interested? We agreed he'd send a tape and a note about himself.

'I was born in Dumbarton in 1953 and am writing songs for some 15 years now. I've lived in Germany for ten years, am married and have three children. I do the odd tour in Switzerland, Holland and of course Germany. Next year Tomas Lynch is going to arrange a couple of gigs in Scotland for me.'

MY SONG OF THE CLYDE

Paul's tape has other good songs—particularly one about the trout and flounder returning to the Clyde

> The River Clyde is rolling strong, I've seen her in her glory.
> I was just a young man then, it's now a different story.
> I've watched the tugs and tankers work, and fight for their survival.
> Seen the QE2 been launched, and welcomed her arrival.

Paul's 'Song Of The Clyde' reawakens a piece of my own childhood, rafts and minnows and the wake of the big ships rolling across the mud flats towards me on the shore.

Sometimes a song can return a memory to us—a moment mislaid then found again as bright and new as the world was then.

MY SONG OF THE CLYDE

Boar-ding the Blue Train at Dum-bar-ton East, loo-king a-round to find a win-dow seat.

Up past the Gas-works and the Bal-lan-tine's geese. I won-der how long they'll sur-vive.

On up past Bow-ling and the great con-crete bridge, Just af-ter Par-tick Glas-gow Docks are in sight

Till we go un-der-ground at Char-ing Cross. This is my song of the Clyde. This is my song of the Clyde.

Long summer evenings on the sand with a flask,
Searching for drift wood to build a raft.
Fishing for minnows with my hands partly clasped,
Wiping the oil from the seat of my pants,
And I was always starvin' when I got back home inside.
This is my song of the Clyde.
This is my song of the Clyde.

Then the radio was playing, there was something in the air
As the great Cargo ships caused their waves to come near.
We'd all jump over them, but I'd stay up in the air
Along with all the gulls that had been following.
There were times I was lost and confused inside.
I'd hang around for the incoming tide.
It's never even left me, it's still here inside.
This is my song of the Clyde.
This is my song of the Clyde.

Words and music by Paul Joses

JIM BROWN

A leading light of the folk music cell in the Cumbernauld Theatre Club, Jim has a very individual and dramatic singing and guitar style, and bases his guitar phrases in some ways on highland piping.

Jim's songs are usually politically committed. There are two of his on the *Glasgow Horizons* album, one about South Africa and the other about seals dying off Scotland's coasts.

He has made several songs about Scotland's loss of its industrial base, and the role of trades unions.

> My old man in his day, to my brothers and me he used to say
> Never let them grind you down,
> Build yer union strong and sound and the boss won't get his way.

But Jim writes local songs too. The 'Vroom Vroom Man' was a wellknown character on Maryhill Road, where 'he used to run about driving an invisible vehicle—I don't know if it was a car or a lorry.'

> When I was a workin lad in dear old Glesga town
> You'd get a winter's mornin when its transport let you down.
> If a tramcar chanced tae jump the rails the way that tramcars can
> You'd feel a touch of envy when you saw the Vroom Vroom Man.
> He'd come oot o the mornin mist just as the sun peeped through,
> Ridin in a motor car not seen by me and you.
> And his engine it was noisy as along the road he'd zoom.
> His thrapple was his throttle as he roared out Vroom Vroom Vroom.
> (Jim's tune is a version of 'Johnson's Motor Car'!)

THE WAVERLEY

Jim works in one of the few yards left on the river. He says that when the Waverley comes past, work stops and everyone waves, because of the pleasure of seeing on the Clyde a last representative of the sea-going paddle steamers that once crowded the water.

The last verse originally ended with

> And the Clyde's tae get a Russian Hydrofoil
> But there's only one WAVERLEY.

There was a report that a Russian hydrofoil was coming to skim the Clyde but it never arrived.

THE WAVERLEY POLKA

Sail-ing doon the Clyde on the Wav- er- ley, a grand old boat is the Wav- er- ley,

She'll take ye doon tae Rothe-say and be back for tea, the way that she did when you were wee.

When the bus- kers played at the aft- er end, the kind of tunes that were the trend,

You were al- ways sure tae meet wi' a friend a- fore you left the quay. Oh

When you watched the paddles going round and round
And heard the engine's thumping sound,
Then your happy young heart would start tae pound
At the thought of reaching the sea.

And the shipyard lads would wave 'hallo'
When building ships was all the go,
With a dozen shipyards in a row
But noo there's barely three.

Now a boat marina soon, they say
For the Glasgow docks where the big ships lay.
Where the rich folk all can sport and play
Wi' their ain wee Waverleys.

And everything is 'North Sea Oil'
Where lads from here have gone tae toil.
But tae that wee boat we'll aye be loyal
'Cos there's only one Waverley.

Words by Jim Brown
Music 'Miss Campbell's Polka'

163

BILL MCVICAR

My father. A man with many gifts. Among them was a love of music, particularly music with a touch of the exotic.

In family gatherings, he was a performer. Songs I learned from his singing included 'My Brother Sylvest' and 'The Darkie Sunday School'. (Which Adam McNaughtan has rewritten as 'The Glasgow Sunday School'.) But my father's party piece was the recitation.

Two favourite pieces were 'Tam O Shanter', and a poem which may have stirred the first sparks of republicanism in me. It begins with clansman MacAllister gathering in his kinsmen with the story of how he once danced before the king, and at the punchline the queen murmurs low to him,

> Och, where was you MacAllister, the night I married him?

I have a German-made concertina which my father bought before I was born. Its bellows are made of paper which now wheezes but can still hold a slow tune. I have the now rather bent and tattered leatherbound volumes of Kipling which first were bought by my father's father.

My father was an engineer. I have inherited from him many things and qualities which I value. But none more valued than my love of music and song, of the magic of words and ideas, and of the great adventure of finding out how things are made and how things work.

WHA SAW THE 42ND and TODAY IS HOGMANAY

My father sang both these songs to us. 'The 42nd' is widely known—correspondence in the Glasgow Herald in 1966 produced various versions. The 42nd were the Black Watch, embarking for foreign wars.

When we lived in Dingwall in the North the tattie howkers would arrive by train from the south—whole classes of underachieving city kids out of school early to earn money lifting potatoes.

I have found no source for the Hogmanay words other than my father, so it should probably be listed in the reference books as 'collected by Wm McG McVicar, Kilbarchan'.

Artie and Cilla of the Singing Kettle recorded it recently, so a song kept alive by my father will now be known to thousands of young Scots.

164

WHA SAW THE 42ND

Wha saw the for-ty se-cond? Wha saw them gaun a-wa? Wha saw the for-ty se-cond mer-chin doon the Broom-ie-law?

) Some o them had tat-tie scones. Some o them had nane at aa. Some o them had a wee drop whis-ky for tae keep the cauld a-wa.
) Some o them had tar-tan toories. Some o them had nane at aa. Some o them had green um-brell-as for tae keep the rain a-wa.

Wha saw the tattie howkers? Wha saw them gaun awa?
Wha saw the tattie howkers merchin doon the Broomielaw.
Some o them had boots and stockins.
Some o them had nane at aa.
Some o them had a wee drop whisky
Fur tae keep the cauld awa.

TODAY IS HOGMANAY

To-day is Hog-ma-nay. To-mor-row's Hog-ma-na-nay. And ah'm gaun up the brae, tae see my I-rish Gran-nie. Ah'll

take her tae a ball. Ah'll take her tae a sup-per, and when ah get her there ah'll stick her nose in the Sing-in but-ter.

Ah- ah ah- ah ah, ah- ah ah- ah ah- ay, ah- ah ah- ah ah, and that's the Gae-lic cho- rus.

(These ah-ahs are bagpipe imitations. You 'sing through your nose' while holding your nose closed with thumb and finger. At the same time you use the first two fingers of your other hand to beat gently and rhythmically on your throat.)

CY LAURIE

A classy traditional singer with a lovely light voice, Cy has enriched the Glasgow folk scene in two ways.

He performs with the group Scotia, alongside legendary fiddler and singer Willy Beaton. Scotia appears on the Lismor *Glasgow Horizons* album.

And Cy runs the Riverside Club, home of song and story, folk concerts and floor-shaking ceilidh dancing, near the heart of old Glasgow.

JAMIE RAEBURN

Cy says he hasn't sung this song in years. His version of the song is combined from three singers he admires. But I recall him singing it and making it completely his own.

For Norman Buchan this song was the exception to the rule that a bad song calls Scotland Caledonia.

A song about the 1837 Glasgow Cotton Spinners strike was set to the tune.

> When first we were arrested, and lodged in Glasgow gaol.
> They stripped us of our clothing, left us naked in our cell.
> No sympathy they showed to us, no not the least ava.
> Because we were united men in Caledonia.

The 'united men' were trades union officials, convicted but pardoned in 1840 after public outcry.

Alasdair Robertson also put a new lyric to the tune.

SONG FOR GLASGOW

> Night-lights on the river partners in the dance
> we're settled here together in the seed-bed of romance
> you've sometimes been a saviour rarely been my curse
> but we can shape the future now for better or for worse
> We've known fears and deprivation in the waste-lands of our dreams
> we've been forged by politicians their dealings and their schemes
> but love's domain is beauty and lovers raise a home
> so I'll celebrate my city in the days that are to come

This tune links the hardships endured by the poor and the partiality of the law, the rise in trade unionism and the struggle for social power for the people, and Glasgow's new optimism and confidence.

JAMIE RAEBURN

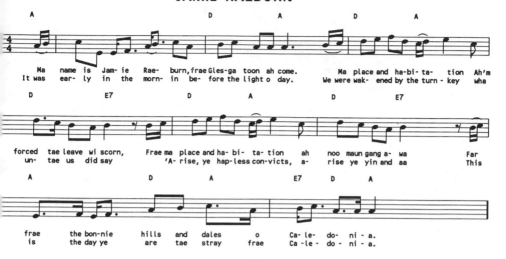

Ma name is Jamie Raeburn, frae Glesga toon ah come.
Ma place and habitation Ah'm forced tae leave wi scorn,
Frae ma place and habitation ah noo maun gang awa
Far frae the bonnie hills and dales o Caledonia.

It was early in the mornin before the light o day.
We were wakened by the turnkey wha untae us did say
'Arise, ye hapless convicts, arise ye yin and aa
This is the day ye are tae stray frae Caledonia.

We aa arose, pit on oor clothes.
Oor herts were full o grief.
Oor freens who stood aroond the coach
Could grant us no relief.
Oor parents, wives, and sweethearts.
Their herts were broke in twa.
Tae see us leave the hills and dales o Caledonia.

Fareweel, ma aged mither.
Ah'm vexed for what ah've done,
Ah hope none will cast up to you
The race that ah hae run.
Ah hope God will protect you
When ah am far awa.
Far frae the bonnie hills and dales o Caledonia.

Farewell, ma honest faither.
You are the best o men,
And likewise ma ain sweethert.
It's Caterin is her name,
Nae mair we'll walk by Clyde's clear stream
Nor by the Broomielaw.
For ah maun leave the hills and dales o Caledonia.

167

'You'll just have to sing them'

The Wee Back Room of the Scotia

A motley crew of folk personages who have not been featured in this book, but who with many others have kept the city singing.

'YOU'LL JUST HAVE TO SING THEM'

The principle of One Singer One Song is to be found in the pubs of Glasgow. Singing folk pubs and pubs that host folk clubs. They develop then fade away as focal points.

Does the singing have to stop, because the pub must shut?

When the Wee Back Room of the Scotia was shut, singing sessions perched for a while on The Wee Man, then settled on the Victoria Bar, known as the Vicky.

Now the Vicky has lost its oomph.

At one point, in those quaint old days when the pubs shut for the afternoon, the Third Eye hosted mighty instrumental sessions, with the occasional song inserted, but the management viewpoint on this changed—we were told our free music might deter people from attending the paid-for evening gigs.

I wish not to offend people involved in the many fine pub music sessions that happen or happened in other venues—the Marland and the Riverside, Heilan Jessies and the Babbity Bowster. I'm writing about the sessions I knew firsthand. The trick is to find the new one while the energy is high and before the people who want to chat to a backdrop of music move in.

When Billy Connolly and Tam Harvey started to drink in the Scotia it was so quiet on a Saturday night they could play dominoes on the bar counter. Then it got so busy you couldn't get in until someone fell out. Then it got quiet again.

Now the Scotia is again providing a platform, not so much the spontaneous sessions of old as a showcase for solo singers and for new writing.

There are always groups performing in Glasgow pubs, by the by, but this book is about the solo singer.

The solo singer was pushed out of the pubs by the plague of fiddlers. Mind, some of my best friends are fiddlers, and mostly they are also mean singers.

Fiddler and Irish piper Jim Daily and I have played in many fiddle-based groups. Groups with names like Robbery With Violins, Ba'Heid McBear, The Black Velvet Band, Sourrocks, Houghmagundie, The Blue Sky Boys and Audio Murphy.

Most notably we had a winter tour of Finland as Glasgow Green, Jim and I and fiddle man cum writer cum frontiersman Seán Damer, plus queen of singers Mary Wall. The crack was mighty and the tunes went on forever. I have a great collection of newspaper clippings. All in Finnish.

So I am in favour of fiddle playing. Very much so. It's just those demons who care for nothing but fiddle playing I can't stand.

The newer breed of fiddle fanatics who came in, intent on speed and dash, and with no time for singing. They compete over knowledge of tunes and speed of execution—the faster the tune the deader the interpretation!

And they stop people listening. Check for yourself. When a gang of fiddlers starts to play, the pub audience will cheer the first number. They applaud the second number. By selection three everyone is so deep in conversation they'll hardly notice the end.

Then try and get a hearing for a song—in fact, some smart individual fiddlers and formal groups I know pace themselves—they get a song going every third time just so they can keep the general noise level down enough to hear themselves on the instrumental numbers.

The fiddler flocks don't care about the punters anyway. They are there for each other - to share knowledge and establish their plucking order.

There are ways to fight the plague of fiddlers.

You could refuse to let them start. Some pub back rooms are taken over for the evening by a group devoted to singing. They don't let fiddle players in.

You can follow the Scotia's recent approach, and make the singing performances more formal. One microphone outranks a dozen bodhrans.

The best counter-attack is the solo virtuoso. An unaccompanied singer with a strong sweet voice will cut through and get the silent audience that no instrumentalist outside a formal concert setting is ever accorded in Glasgow.

The silence cows the fiddlers for a moment, but they'll be savaging another 90 mph reel before applause dies away, so you'd better have another singer warmed up at the side of the track and ready to run.

If you can ensure that the next singer starts a strong-going chorus song you may change the course of the night. Who knows? You might even get the fiddlers joining in!

171

ALL THE TUNES IN THE WORLD

I was sitting beside Iain Mackintosh one afternoon in the Star Club. An instrumental group began to play the Irish tune 'The South Wind'. Iain and I sang along to the tune, and we both said 'There ought to be words.'
I began to think about Jim Daily, fiddler and piper and friend, who would get me into trouble—at the end of a night, after 'time' had been bawled Jim would keep playing tunes. The publican would appeal to me since there was obviously no use in speaking to Jim.

So I'd say 'Jim, that had to be the last tune.' And Jim would answer 'Fine—did you ever hear this tune called 'Around The House And Mind The Dresser'? He'd play that one. Then another called 'When Sick Is It Tea You Want?' Then three more.

Eventually he'd be cajoled into laying his fiddle down. Sighs of relief all round.

Then Jim would say 'Do you know 'Paddy In The Smoke'? It goes Diddle dyah did daddle de, dow diddy ah dum—' and away he'd go again.

I wrote my song quickly. It was premiered for a group of Irish hikers passing through the Vicky Bar. Then a couple of months later at the Folk Festival on Glasgow Green I lay on the grass to listen to Iain do a lovely set of songs. After he finished he came and sat beside me.

'Iain, I wrote that song to the 'South Wind' tune.' I sang it quietly in his ear. He looked at me, a little startled.

'I'll sing that!' he said.

This song is for all the other people who ought to be in this book.

The songwriters that I couldn't get a direct connecting Glasgow song for, or I couldn't get permission for the song, or whose songs don't quite fit into the style of this book, or who met all the rules but there wasn't space enough eg Sean Tierney, John Martyn, Nancy Dangerfield, Alan Tall, Ian Walker, Ian Bruce, Peter Nardini, Danny Kyle, Dave Anderson.

The Glasgow musicians and singers who love the music and the songs - many many of them—I'll just name some of the ones I've played in groups with and learned about music from—Jim Daily, Maggy Faulds, Seán Damer, Gerry McIlwhinnie, Carol Sweeney, Willy Beaton, Harry Bickerstaff, Mary Wall, Shuggie MaGuinness, Mick Murphy, John Dillon.

There are, you'd not lift an eyebrow now to learn, differing versions of this last song about.

This is my version.

ALL THE TUNES IN THE WORLD

Lay down the bor-rowed gui- tar, lay down the fidd- le and bow. You'd like one more drink at the bar

but the man- a- ger says you must go. CH All the tunes in the world are dan- cing a-round in your head

but the clock on the gan-try says play-time is done, you'll just have to sing them in- stead.

Lay down the jig and the reel,
Lay down the planxty and slide.
Everyone knows how you feel
But there's no time to take one more ride.

The barmaid has put on her coat,
The barman has emptied the slops,
The manager's pals are afraid
That the music might bring in the cops.

Everyone here feels the same.
Yes, you deserve one more tune.
But you know the rules of the game.
It's time to go howl at the moon.

Words by Ewan McVicar
Music 'The South Wind'
Published by Gallus Music

GLOSSARY

airt—direction
ba' on the slates—game's up
baggy minnies—big minnows
bampot—heedless fool, nutter
barley bree—whisky
bauchle—a down-at-heel person
bauchlin'—shuffling
bawbee—half-penny
berkie—a berserk outburst
bevvy—beverage
bide—stay
blate—diffident
blethered—talked idly
bogie (game's a bogie)—game's off
bree / brey—cooking liquid
breenge—rush
broo—unemployment bureau / benefit office
cadge a hudgie—catch a lift on the back of a
    vehicle
callants—youths
cast up to—reproach by reminding
channty—chamber pot
chickie mellie—street game
clachan—village
clairt—muck, mess
cleek—iron hook
close—entry to a tenement's common stair
cludgie—lavatory
crack—entertaining talk
crans—cranes
crousely—arrogantly
didgy—dustbin
dings—strikes
doon the wattair—down the river (Clyde)
dreep(noun)—'drip', bland, passive person
dreep aff a dyke—hang by the fingertips from the
    top of a wall and drop down
dunny—basement in a tenement
dyers' clugs—wooden shoes worn by dyers
fiere—fere, comrade
foregaither—meet
gallus—bold, cheeky
gantry—bottle stand in a bar, framework for
    heavy loads
gar—make
gas in a peep (put someone's)—cut someone
    down to size
gaun—going, operating
geans—wild cherries
gird—iron hoop
glaikit—foolish, stupid
Glasgow Magistrate—herring
guernsey—heavy jumper
gutty boots—rubber boots
haderums—bagpipes
hauders-on—riveters' mates

heelster gowdy—head over heels
hirstlin'—slithering
hoodies—hooded crows
hunch, cuddy, hunch—street game, trial of
    strength
hurl—ride in a wheeled vehicle
hurly chair—wheelchair
jawbox—sink
jeelly jaurs—jam jars
jorrie—jaurie, marble
kick the can—street game, like hide and seek
lawin'—tavern bill
loanins—pastures
lugs—ears
lum hat—top hat, chimney hat
Macallums—icecreams with raspberry sauce
mavis—song-thrush
mellin'—hammering
melt—spleen / strike in that area
mind—remember
nyaff—wee impudent nonentity
peerie—top
peever—hopscotch
planxty—tune for the Irish harp
plukes—pimples
pokes—paper bags
pooches—pockets
reivers—raiders
roch—rough
rottans—rats
sannies—sandshoes, gymshoes (like trainers)
sclimmin—climbing
shilpit—starved-looking
single-end—one-roomed flat
slide—Irish polka
soughs—makes a sighing, rushing sound
spelding—split, dried fish
stank—gutter
staun their lane—stand alone
steamie—public wash-house
stour—dust, commotion
strides—trousers
tak tent—take notice
tally men—debt collectors
tattie howkers—potato gatherers
term-time—fixed date to start and end of farm
    employment
terr—spree
teuchter—Highlander (jocular term)
thrang—busy
tottie scones—potato scones
totties—potatoes
wally close—tiled close
yont—beyond

174

PEOPLE

175

SONGS